Stories of HOPE Australia

Reviews and Testimonials

"Stories of HOPE is a life-changing experience and now you can take a piece of it home with you. Stepping into the worlds of these everyday heroes will empower and inspire you to know anything is possible in your own life. I can honestly say that it was HOPE that took me from darkness to light."

Donna Thistlethwaite, suicide survivor and Stories of HOPE storyteller

"Stories of HOPE is a powerful and emotive read. The various shared lived experience stories hit home that no matter what adversity life can throw at us, HOPE is always the bright light needed to never give up!"

Simon Gillard, inspirational speaker and bestselling author of Life Sentence: A Police Officer's Battle with PTSD Penguin Random House 2017.

"Kerrie Atherton is the embodiment of what it means to create community in today's busy culture that emphasises Instagram, highlight reels, and shiny appearances. Now more than ever, so many of us feel lost and alone and Kerrie's work illuminates the authentic experience that connects all of us. Stories of HOPE is a fast-growing movement of people coming together to celebrate life in all of its trials, to feel heard, and to contribute their truth to those who need to hear it most. I am personally honoured to have had my life blessed by Kerrie; she has the gift of making everyone feel welcomed and wanted in this world. Her ripple effect is the antithesis of modern day media, the antidote to the isolation epidemic, and the future that we want our children to live."

Monique Parker, Communications Manager Media & PR Tourism Marketing Kingfisher Bay Resort group

"From the moment I met Kerrie Atherton, I knew she was special. Warm, caring, genuine and sincere, this woman was born to help others. By sharing her own difficult past including drug and alcohol addiction and suicidal thoughts, Kerrie is testament to the strength of the human spirit and proof that with the right mindset we can turn our life around. Kerrie changes lives by sharing the stories of others who have found hope in the darkest of times through her organisation Stories of Hope. This book is a compilation of 12 of those stories that will change the way you think forever".

Ingrid Nelson, Editor In Chief with Profile Magazine

*To anyone who feels like they need
HOPE this book is for you.*

STORIES OF HOPE AUSTRALIA

Everyday people, extraordinary stories

KERRIE ATHERTON

Stories of HOPE Australia: Everyday people, extraordinary stories
Author – Kerrie Atherton
© Kerrie Atherton 2019

www.storiesofhope.com.au
info@storiesofhope.com.au

This book is sold with the understanding that the author is not offering specific personal advice to the reader. For professional advice, seek the services of a suitable, qualified practitioner. The author disclaims any responsibility for liability, loss or risk, personal or otherwise, that happens as a consequence of the use and application of any of the contents of this book.

All rights reserved. This book may not be reproduced in whole or part, stored, posted on the internet, or transmitted in any form or by any means, electronic, mechanical, photocopying, recording, or other, without permission from the author of this book.

ISBN: 978-0-9876436-0-5

Foreword

I first had the pleasure of chatting with Kerrie Atherton on my radio show, *Coffee Chats with Matt Collins*. Kerrie's contagious passion and energy were an obvious presence in our conversation. During our chat, Kerrie shared some of the family challenges she endured as a child which extended far beyond the usual mild family issues that most first world families face, including my own. What I realised about this strong woman was that these past events have not defined who she is now.

In my time as a radio host, I have shared conversations with people from all walks of life, from priests to prostitutes, singers to sports stars, the terminally ill to the totally unbelievable, but what stood out for me when I chatted with Kerrie was her empathy. She has a way of finding hope in every situation. And that is exactly what Kerrie and her remarkable friends have done with this book, *Stories of HOPE*.

All of the stories you are about to read are remarkable. Like me, you will need to remind yourself these are true life stories and not scenes from a Hollywood movie. Since our conversation, Kerrie and I have become good friends.

I'm confident that others will agree: Kerrie is the type of friend every person longs for; the type of friend who is always there for you regardless of how good or bad life is going. Regardless of whether you have just received your annual tax check or you are down to your last dollar. Regardless of whether you have just met the person of your dreams or you have just been through a messy break-up. Regardless of whether you have just welcomed a new little human into the world or if you have just said your final goodbye to someone you treasured.

Regardless of anything, Kerrie is that friend who is always there. When I am surrounded by people like that, it makes me want to be a better person. That positivity snowballs. It's inevitable. Good breeds good.

And so it is with this book; the people behind the stories in this book have shown tremendous resilience, courage, bravery and persistence to overcome their individual challenges. Like children's laughter, their stories are contagious.

I invite anyone going through tough times to pick up this book and after only a few pages you will start to feel more confident and gain some clarity towards the best way to face your specific challenge. Let's face it, if you have already picked up this book there is presumably at least one small issue you are dealing with, and that is nothing to be ashamed of. In fact, if you have some issues in your life, let me welcome you to the club. The "I have some issues" club. There's only about seven billion of us. Remind me to get you a badge.

The stories in this book stand as a reminder that we all have our issues. If everyone put their problems in a bowl, you would very quickly take yours back out again. I truly believe that. Not only do I believe it, it is simply a fact. There is always someone struggling more than you. Even if it doesn't always seem like it.

This is why it is so important to share your challenges. Share with people you trust. Maybe they won't understand. Maybe they won't get it. Maybe they won't be able to relate and that's okay.

I am no expert in psychology but I can tell you this much: I have chatted with hundreds of people on my show and each and every single one who overcame massive hurdles said they talked to someone. All of them. Not one or two of them. Not some of them. Each and every one of them said that sharing their story with someone else helped them to overcome their struggles.

Are you getting it?

It's important to share what is going on for you. Regardless of how insignificant you may think it is, tell someone about it. A

Foreword

problem shared is a problem halved. That's why you are going to get so much out of this book. A collection of people who are just like you and me who have been brave enough to share their sad, uncomfortable, sometimes tragic but always inspiring stories.

Congratulations on picking up this book. The pages ahead are sure to remind you that you can overcome any challenge you may be facing no matter how severe, intense or tragic it may seem right now.

Now it's over to Kerrie and her remarkable friends.

Matt Collins Radio talk show host Coffee Chats with Matt Collins, and newspaper journalist.

Contents

Foreword ix

From a lightbulb moment a vision grew xv

Kerrie Atherton
The Girl Who Broke Through: The founder of
Stories of HOPE Australia 1

Mark John Castro
From Heartache to Hero: A grieving father finds
purpose in teaching disadvantaged kids boxing 21

Leonie Fay Mulgrew
An Unbreakable Spirit: The transformation from
child abuse victim to radiant survivor 33

Dave Larkin
Home is Where the Heart is: Homelessness
doesn't discriminate 41

Stuart Rawlins
From Top Dog to The Black Dog and Back Again:
The story of one of the leading investigators in
Australia's biggest murder investigation –
the Daniel Morcombe case 49

Trudi Bareham
Stepping Through the Lyme Life: My story of
surviving Lyme disease 71

Darron Eastwell
One Life-Changing Moment: The day I broke my brain 83

Shelley Ross May
Learning to Love Yourself: The truth about my
battle with bulimia 91

Denise Dielwart
Healing grief, one widow at a time 99

Luke Bourne
Bourne For a Greater Purpose: The battle against
one of the world's rarest cancers. 109

Angela Williams
Fearless for Freedom's Sake: From self-discovery
to selfless crusader 119

Stephen Dale
Bouncing Back When You Hit Rock Bottom:
From devastating accident to motivational leader..................129

Acknowledgements 145

From a lightbulb moment a vision grew...

There is a venue on the Sunshine Coast where lives are transformed on the same night on the same week of every month. This is Stories of HOPE, which began with a simple idea linked with a big vision to spread the strongest message to anyone who is going through a challenge in life – the message that they are not alone and that they are loved.

It was 2017 when Kerrie Atherton reached out to a small group of friends, finally daring to share her vision to offer a brighter future to those who needed to hear a message of HOPE. Kerrie dreamed of reaching not only her local community on the Sunshine Coast, but also the state of Queensland and branching out to all of Australia ... maybe even the world. As she waited, sitting alone on a chair, the time she had set for this, her milestone event, was drawing near. But nobody had arrived.

Kerrie began to entertain the thought she might be left in the room with just her husband for company that night and her dream might come crashing down before it had been given the chance to take flight. But then, as if in slow motion, thirty people walked through the door, one after the other. This was it, her dream had just become a reality.

This is where Stories of HOPE Australia began.

Now, a little room in the Sands Tavern in Maroochydore becomes a place where people regularly come together for a common purpose, to find and to give HOPE. Many are broken, many have been through such devastating circumstances, many feel alone in their suffering, but this is a sacred place where they know they can instantly belong, with the knowledge that others have been where they are and understand what they are going through. People who know their pain and people who have stories of victory can testify to the fact that there is a light at the end of every tunnel and that HOPE is possible.

Stories of HOPE Australia has given a voice to those who have taken to the stage to share their heart-wrenching and inspirational stories and it has provided a catalyst for transformation in those who attend to hear them. Everyone leaves the monthly event changed for the better, with a new sense of purpose and destiny they never dreamed to be possible.

This is the power of Stories of HOPE and at the beginning of each chapter, Kerrie shares the journey that led her to meet each of the remarkable people featured. Here, they share their personal stories through this humble, but incredibly powerful, platform.

Kerrie Atherton

The Girl Who Broke Through:
The founder of Stories of HOPE Australia

A STORY OF A PILL-ADDICTED
AND ALCOHOLIC GIRL

Her messed up life.
Her recovery.
And her ongoing journey to divert others from the path she has walked.

Each of us has a past. Some have suffered more trauma than others. But for us to live a worthwhile life, one must move past the point of being a victim and into that of being a victor. There, a wonderful future awaits. I never chose the path life had for me. I always dreamed of being a famous jazz musician, just like my grandfather and my father. Or an actress on the big stage with all the lights and beautiful costumes to be adored by many for the quirky colourful person I was on the inside. But fate had other plans.

For many years, I felt ripped off, but I never knew what great future lay around the corner. At the time, it felt more like a very long and winding road, but in the scheme of life, it was still a corner.

Having said that, I would not change the experiences I had to endure, even though they were filled with much sadness, trauma, depression, anxiety and many triggers, to lead to the life I live today. Because of the path my life took, I have been privileged to be walking alongside the most broken of broken, the most unloved and judged of society, and even the rich and famous who appear to have it all, but are just like the rest of us on the inside, emotions in skin with invisible scars.

These experiences have led me into the tribe of the wounded and gifted me with a rare ability to empathise with those who have suffered on the deepest level. I have been privy to some of the darkest secrets of those who have never dared to bare their soul to anyone. But someone like me, who has walked the path they have, just gets what they are going through.

To be able to have come out the other end of the trials I have faced empowered and full of victory, much stronger in capacity and much richer in spirit than before, and to be able to bring HOPE to those on the journey in their darkest moments, gives me joy that's indescribable and something that no amount of money could ever buy. To be able to play a small part in helping change the life of another for good is a gift often only earned by suffering and the ability to overcome. To have had the privilege of deep relationships on a heart connection far beyond the menial talk of weather, and to see the beauty in the smallest of things, has enabled me to learn deep gratitude. I am the girl who broke through.

"I am an extraordinarily strange girl living in the midst of ordinary circumstances," was what I thought at the time. But looking back now, I was an ordinary and very complex girl living in extraordinarily tumultuous circumstances.

Seeing my father cry for the first time was devastating to me. It was as if a tragedy had happened. It was just an argument! Many of which he and I'd had before. How could I be so awful that I had made my father cry? What I didn't know then was that my father was almost at rock bottom. Watching my mum grapple daily with alcoholism was becoming too much for him to bear. It would have been much easier for him if I just did as I was told. But I was a rebel and even from an early age, no matter how hard I tried to comply, nobody was going to tell me what to do.

The fact that Dad would go off to work each morning, leaving his depressed wife with us three young children, and not knowing if he would come home to any of us being alive (due to my mum's depression) had taken its toll. It wasn't my fault, just another episode in the daily struggle of life that would tip him over the edge. I loved my dad so much and seeing him cry broke my heart.

"Hey Kerrie Anne, what's your game now can anybody play?" A very average but catchy tune that came out in the '60s. My name is Kerrie Anne, so it had a lasting and comforting effect when my dad would playfully sing it to me. But my life wasn't anything like a game and more like a charade. Never feeling like I fit in, but more like an alien with two heads, preschool was my first real taste of social life on the outside and it was a frightening place.

The truth is that I would have loved to have had many friends to play games with me, but I felt totally alone in the big wide world. My only refuge in those early years was amidst the calm chaos of my home with my family, but particularly time spent with my dad, with whom I'd always had a close connection. We had a lot in common. He had also grown up with an alcoholic mother. I was born on the same day as his father (also an alcoholic). He had been an alcoholic. I was yet to become an alcoholic. He was musical. I was musical. We were creatives. We spoke a silent code. Who would have thought that the words to songs just like *Hey Kerrie Anne* could have such a lasting impact and pierce through a world spiralling out of control to bring moments of such joy and happiness in the midst of turmoil?

Three of us little terrors under three by the age of twenty-three: that was my mother's lot. She had so much love for my two brothers and I though, even if it was extremely tough. Never really feeling connected to her own parents or siblings, she finally had a family of her own. What she didn't want was the effects of depression, the devastating effects of alcoholism or the suicidal thoughts that constantly plagued her daily existence. Mum did her best. To the outside world, she appeared to have it all. Stunning looks, money, a loving husband who had a great sales job by day and who was a jazz musician by night and us three angel kids. She worked through the day, made many of our clothes, baked cookies and cakes, taught me to knit and sew, and was a referee for the constant fighting between my brothers and me.

There didn't seem to be anything she didn't or couldn't do. Mum loved interior decorating, often jazzing up our home and redecorating her best friend's house. She was also an intellectual genius. In fact, looking from the outside, she was super-mum. But something was wrong! She lacked the cognitive ability to emotionally cope, as not only was she an alcoholic with many triggers, she also suffered from manic depression.

Dad would come home from work sometimes and Mum would drive off. We would all hop in the car with Dad and drive around looking for her, often to find her parked in her car down near the water near our home, crying. There were nights when I wouldn't see my mum. When I would ask dad "Where's Mum?" he would often reply, "She's sick." I now know, on those nights she was locked away in her bedroom drinking and as my young years rolled by, things were getting worse and worse.

One sunny afternoon, I had a sudden and desperate desire to wear my favourite purple dress. I approached my mum, who was in the laundry doing the washing, and I barely had the words out of my mouth when she screamed and started shaking. She was being electrocuted with both hands stuck behind the washing machine. As I ran screaming to my brothers who were in the lounge room, we all huddled together jumping up and down on the lounge crying hysterically. I was seven and my brothers were six and four. We thought that was the last time we would ever see her.

After being taken to the neighbours' for the night, we came home the next day to see our mum had survived. Burns up both wrists, but alive. I was so happy to see her again. Mum later told me that when she was electrocuted, her whole life flashed before her eyes. She was being led by a man through the most beautiful park she had ever seen and asked if she would go with him. Her reply was, "I have to go back to look after my three young children." God gave her back to us for many years to come.

It was December 12, 1972 and I was excited about our holiday to Port Macquarie. We would be basking in the summer sun by the idyllic palm trees, or so I thought. My brother's eighth birthday was two days away. We had just arrived at the holiday cabins and it was going to be a great family holiday. I was nine. Never will I forget it. Nine. This was the event that changed the course of my life forever and was the catalyst that held me captive to debilitating fear for many years into my adult life.

> This was the event that changed the course of my life forever.

Dad had checked in at the front desk and given the owner our address, phone number, car rego and anything else they needed to track you down should you do a runner and not pay the bill at the end of the stay. There were no credit cards back then, so a deposit was paid at the beginning and the rest at the end. But, little did we know that when we arrived we would not be staying long.

Later that day, as I played with my new friend that I had only just met in the playground, *he* turned up. I was playing on the swing and this new friend said to me, "I'm going to introduce you to my friend Max." I had remarkable intuition at that age because something told me he was bad. I froze, as I tried to get out the words, "I do not want to meet him." Before I could, she had said to him, "Max this is Kerrie." I had an eerie feeling come over me and I felt the hair on the back of my neck rise.

The next morning, December 13, I awoke so excited about my brother's birthday being the next day. Our family made a very big deal out of birthdays. I could hear the patter of rain on the roof outside and realised that if the rain continued, there may not be much to do. I wanted my brother to have a great birthday, so I ventured outside to the tourist attractions notice board located on the wall of the carport adjacent to our cabin to see what options we had. After all, I was the self-appointed family fixer. It was my responsibility to make sure everyone was happy.

Standing looking at the billboard I suddenly sensed an evil presence behind me. I turned around and there *he* was. He seemed to be towering over me like a giant. I was only nine and quite small. I couldn't escape. Pinning me against the wall, he exposed himself to me and tried to violate me with his hands. I couldn't move. I was frozen with fear. When he realised I was an unwilling participant, for some strange reason he left me alone, but not without a final warning that I had better not tell anyone. Maybe he thought someone was coming, I don't know, but he had left an internal scar on me that would not be erased for years.

I ran inside and revealed to my parents the horror that I had just experienced. They drove me straight to the police station and I had to go through the humiliation of revealing the events to a policeman, who was yet another stranger to me. The officer made a comment about the perpetrator being the son of the owner of the holiday cabins, who was in his early twenties. From the discussion my parents had with the officer, they had a sense that I was not the first victim of this paedophile. With that, the officer announced that if we wanted to press charges, my parents would have to bring me back up to Port Macquarie to give evidence in court and I would have to relive my nightmare all over again. The policeman's words were, "I don't think you should put your daughter through that trauma; she is too young."

We packed up immediately and left, going back down to Sydney. Travelling back home with me was not only shame and devastation at what had just happened, but absolute fear with the knowledge that he knew where I lived and that we had been to the police. In my mind, he would be coming to get me. My nightmare had just begun.

From that day on, I lived in constant terror. I was a prisoner in my own home. I grew to hate the darkness. It represented fear of the unknown and frightening times. It was the middle of summer and I would lie in my bed at night waiting for the noise at my window. I refused from that day to ever sleep with the windows open because then he could get me. I would sweat in the sweltering heat with no air coming in or going out. As the months rolled on, my fear turned from him coming to get me, to someone, anyone, coming to get me and attacking me in my home.

Upon arriving home from going anywhere, no matter what time of the day it was, I would check my wardrobe and under my bed to make sure a stranger hadn't entered and was hiding lying in wait to attack me. As the sun went down, and the darkness of the nights closed in, my heart would pound, my stomach was constantly sick, I felt like a raw exposed nerve with no protection. I was petrified.

School at that time was no haven for me either. A place that is meant to be fun, carefree and filled with friendships, a kind of a respite for many kids from whatever hell is going on at home, had become yet another place of fear for me. I felt so different to the other kids, as though I had come from another planet even. I must have worn the invisible sign on my head that said *victim*, as I was alienated by other children, and my teacher at the time seemed to hate me. At one stage, she put her hands around my throat and made a half-hearted gesture to choke me in front of the class, just to crush my already-humiliated spirit. This wasn't to be the only incident; I also experienced other severe forms of bullying at the hands of another teacher at this school.

I couldn't work out what was wrong with me. Was I just too ordinary or somehow extraordinarily weird? Or was I bad? I couldn't work out the answers to these questions in my young mind. The only people that seemed to accept me were my parents and brothers. But when I got home from school, my mum was becoming more and more of a prisoner to the vices of alcohol and she often became manic, screaming at us and then not talking to us for hours. Besides this, my dad was hitting breaking point. I felt totally alone.

Playing the piano was, I think, one of my saving graces. It was a friend to me. One I could reach out to who would not reject me. One who listened to my heartache and to whom I could express my deep sadness. One who was in harmony with me. I would escape for hours and lose myself in melody. As the years went by, I would spend thousands of hours playing songs with my dad as he played the saxophone. We connected over music from an early age and that connection grew stronger and stronger.

Not long after I had been molested, mum decorated my room for me in a desperate attempt to try and make me feel safe and happy in my little haven of terror. I had purple wallpaper, a purple fluffy stool and this mainly purple multi-coloured blanket. My room looked beautiful, but there was one problem. My room was the room next to the road, which was a four-lane highway, and at any time, *he* could turn up and smash the windows and take me. Terror became my constant companion. I still have the multi-coloured blanket today and although I have a vague fondness for it, it is a reminder of the mental torment that I fell victim to. Life was too much for me, now a girl almost ten years of age.

One night as I was getting ready to go to sleep, I checked under my bed as I had already done about ten times, but every time I pulled my head back up, the patterns and colours on the blanket would flash before my eyes and torment me. Everything was spinning out of control and I didn't know what was happening. I now know that I was having a breakdown. Unable to cope with the torment in my head and the constant trauma of the past two years, my mum's near-electrocution, her alcoholism, her depression, the molestation and the bullying at school, not to mention my little brother's best friend who had been tragically run over by a semi-trailer and crushed on our road after school, my little world came crashing down all around me. I couldn't get up. I couldn't move. All I could do was curl up in a ball in the foetal position under my bed and sob uncontrollably.

As if things weren't already hard enough for my family, here I was, my mum and dad's little girl having a breakdown right before their very eyes. My mum came in and picked me up and cradled me. They were helpless. My mum and dad were seeing a psychiatrist at the time and they didn't know what else to do for me. They took me to visit him. As psychiatrists often do, and I don't know what else he could have done as I was in bad shape, he put me on antidepressants and anti-anxiety medication. Antidepressants at ten!

This was going to be the start of a progressive downhill slide. At the time, it appeared as if I was getting some relief from the demons in my head. I seemed to be getting better. But what my parents were not aware of, was the fact that I clung to these tablets as if my very life depended on them and eventually started lying to them to get more. I seemed to be losing them very frequently. My pill addiction had just started and was spiralling quickly. So was my life. I can remember often banging my head into the wall in my bedroom because I hated myself so much. I don't know when this deep-seated sense of self-loathing came in, but my guess is the feeling of worthlessness was constantly reinforced through ongoing bullying at school.

Depression and suicidal thoughts plagued me. I spent many nights going to sleep wishing I wouldn't wake up and then when I did, not knowing how I could possibly get through another day. Then, bingo, I discovered alcohol. I was fifteen, and my first drink was a cask of wine that my brothers had hidden in thirty-degree heat under the caravan across the road. All alone, I drank and washed away all the feelings of sadness, hopelessness, shame and unworthiness. When I had alcohol, I felt on top of the world and I felt like it coloured me in. My new best friend had just arrived and with alcohol, I would never feel abnormal or abandoned again.

Not long after, I met my first boyfriend. He was a seventeen-year-old bodybuilder with tattoos, a pierced ear and a black mullet which was spiked on top. An extremely interesting haircut indeed. My dad instantly detested him. Nevertheless, life seemed wonderful. I would now no longer be the fat girl, the school dork who was continually mocked, picked on and alienated. In the December school holidays my friend taught me how to do hair and makeup and I lost about ten kilograms. While my boyfriend and I were at the movies one day, we bumped into the two coolest girls from my school, Monte Sant' Angelo Catholic Girls College. All of a sudden, when I returned to Year Ten, with my new image intact, I was an instant hit - but with the wrong crowd.

After about six months into Year Ten, everyone I knew was telling me I had a problem with alcohol. How could this possibly be? I had only been drinking for a few months and it made me happy. I thought everyone must be wrong. But then I would hear the stories the day after a big night of drinking about how my personality drastically changed when I was drunk, and I was starting to become extremely depressed when I wasn't drinking. The days after a big night felt like hell on earth. Pills were losing their effect and I thought all I needed to do was ramp up my drinking to a new level, in an attempt to feel the same euphoria and escapism from the pain of reality that I felt when I first started. Even though I had a family history of alcoholism, with my dad having been in AA for years and my mum becoming sober when I was twelve, I thought there was *no way* I could be an alcoholic. After all, I was only sixteen.

I felt so worthless and desperately wanted to feel as though I was worth something to someone – anyone –and the pain of the rejection I felt, caused me to constantly scream out in my head to God, "Why did You even cause me to be born?" Filled with so much hate for myself, I continued smashing my head into walls because I believed I was damaged goods and deserved to be damaged. It also bought a weird sense of relief. After fifteen months, the relationship with my first boyfriend was over. He was more of a hostage and a receptor, kind of an emotional boxing bag for me to unleash all the years of my emotional turmoil on, someone who I thought could fill the endless empty void in my soul and finally make me feel worthwhile. Well, I was wrong.

After parting ways with this boyfriend and nursing my broken heart, I had made a comment to my mum that I was, "going to get someone heaps better than him next time." That statement didn't hold up very well because next, I picked the brother of the head of a well-known biker gang. If my self-esteem was not low enough at the start of this three-month relationship, it was lower than a snake's belly by the end of it and I would go on to have scars for the rest of my life as a result.

My quest for someone better than the previous two relationships went on. I was just trying to fill the deep void inside with a different relationship, a different job in a different location. But I now know all alcoholics go through this. "Geographicals," we call them. But the reality is every time I moved geographically, I would just take myself with me - so nothing changed. Then the blackouts started. I started waking up in strange places. I started feeling shame and embarrassment because I didn't know what happened the night before. Everything was black. I started dressing in black. I turned into a goth. Every second word that came out of my mouth was the F-word. I was in a very dark place. Wanting to die, but too scared to kill myself. The madness continued.

I reluctantly went to the occasional AA meeting to silence my critics (my parents, their friends and my boyfriends). I had heard older sober members say repeatedly as they pointed at me, "I wish I had found this when I was your age." This attention was the last thing I wanted in a million years while I was trying my best to be invisible. My fear of humiliation was debilitating. Everyone at the meetings seemed like they were about a hundred years old and I couldn't possibly imagine that in just two short years, this would be my nightly reality and the highlight of my life.

These people fascinated me though. Even though they all seemed old, they were from all walks of life. From politicians, to pilots and doctors, everyday people mixed with the homeless just in off the streets. They had been to the depths of despair. Places that terrified me. Jail and mental institutions – some had been given electric shocks. Many, due to their addictions, had lost their families. Some had killed and maimed people or harmed themselves, but most of all they had all lost their way. They had lost themselves and every ounce of dignity that they possessed. This was their last stop! And many went out to drink again and never came back.

Everything they said in AA rang in my ears, but I was young and smart and wasn't ready to give up unless I absolutely came to my own rock bottom. Then, when I was seventeen, the unthinkable happened. I had already had a couple of close encounters with death while drunk and under the influence of pills. I had put myself in some dangerous situations, but this rocked my world and catapulted me into the darkest despair and total loss of all self-esteem.

I had seen him before, but only briefly. Yet he caught my eye. His name was Brian. He looked a lot classier than the previous guys I had gone out with and he went to the Catholic Church I had attended for a few years with my father and brothers. My mum came with us at Easter and Christmas. I think she felt doing that was like an insurance policy – she was covered. I only wanted to be loved. At seventeen, I desperately wanted to meet Mr Right. So, one day he finally noticed me and asked me out. I was excited because I really did think that he was different and that I was on the up and up with this guy.

One date. It only took one date to devastate me. We were going to the drive-in and he brought wine. As usual, I could not stop at one drink because I was an alcoholic. As we were leaving, he announced to me that he would be driving me out to the bush alongside a university deserted at night, to rip my clothes off and rape me. I couldn't believe what I was hearing and never believed in a million years that would be true. I thought it was some kind of a sick, disturbing joke. But as we started driving, even in my intoxicated state, I realised that we were not going in the direction of my home and my heart sank. I had rendered myself helpless. He was serious. And that is exactly what happened.

How could I have been so wrong? What did I do to deserve this? Well I thought, I was drunk; maybe it was my fault after all. A lie entered my mind that night that many young girls tell themselves these days to try and ease some of the pain, anger, shame and guilt. Anything to avoid going head to head with these thugs in court and having to relive it all over again with the chance that the judge might come to the decision that I deserved it.

This event has been one of the hardest for me to live with because I never got the chance to stand up for myself. This person dropped me off at my front door afterwards a sobbing mess, like I was a worthless piece of human garbage. He will never get justice for what he did, and I was probably one of many he did it to. I was only able to deal with the shame of this event at the age of forty-nine. I felt so ripped off because for all those years, I hung my head and just never knew my worth. I always felt less than. I know today that God is my vindicator and I know that I am worthy and it was not my fault. Today I can hold my head up high, but it took a long time and much pain and shame to come to this realisation.

After that, I met an ally. Another alcoholic. But this boyfriend was abusive and physically attacked me while we were on holidays. After I got home from this holiday, I was done. I was totally depleted. How did my life so tragically end up like this? Alone and in a total state of depression and hopelessness, I planned to end my life by suicide. Suddenly, I heard a loud voice from up above say, "Don't do it. If you hold on a bit longer, you will find happiness one day." I picked up the phone and called AA instead. I never believed that at eighteen I would throw in the towel, but since that day I have not picked up a drink of alcohol or taken substances to change my mood.

That was thirty-seven years ago. I did, however, get instantly involved in a relationship with an extremely sick, abusive human being and stayed in that relationship for three years. This time, I was like the hostage. I was screamed at on almost a daily basis and was emotionally abused while things were smashed around me day in and day out. I honestly do not know how I managed to stay sober through those three years, but in AA I had a great support network. That is something everyone needs to sustain positive changes in their life. I finally got the courage to leave that relationship and felt free for the first time in my life. I met my husband one year later and we have been married now for thirty-one years.

> I was determined not to be defeated by my past.

Since the day I got sober, I have had a burning passion and desire to help not only change the lives of others but to save as many lives as possible. To use my pain for others' gain and prevent as many young people as

I could from going through what I went through. I still had a long journey of emotional recovery ahead, but I was determined not to be defeated by my past. I was no longer a victim. Always empathetic by nature, I have a deep care for others going through pain. Nobody really understands what it is like to be hurt unless they have walked the journey of suffering also.

When I look at the life I have today, to think I nearly took that away by committing suicide makes me so very sad. I could never have imagined in my wildest dreams what great journey lay just around the corner. And a life lived for the benefit of others is the greatest life we can live. I never would have imagined that I would go on to be able to connect with so many people from around the world, and help change so many lives for good. That I would be able to walk beside my hubby of thirty-one years even through all my brokenness and be the kind of wife that would make him proud simply because of my ability to be able to rise up and overcome and achieve my dreams. Despite how I entered the journey of motherhood, that I would also go on to raise two of the most amazing humans possible and be the kind of mum these days who my daughter and son are proud to call their mother. I also never thought I would have the incredible joy of being a grandmother so early in life.

I have spoken and shared my story at thousands of AA meetings in different locations in Australia and in America. I have counselled and mentored thousands of people of all ages and from all walks of life. My driving passion has been to work with young people and help them not end up where I ended up. As a result of wanting to be a constant in the lives of so many kids who felt they didn't have a consistent role model in their life, I held the position as the founding chaplain in one of the largest state schools in Queensland. Even under the most immense opposition for almost six years, I continued week after week, month after month. I stayed there for the ones. It really is all about the ones. If you can change one person's life, you just don't know what a world-changer that one person is going to go on to be.

I have written several programs where I have shared the experiences of my life and my resiliency and determination for survival. These have been presented in schools throughout Queensland and helped change the lives of many students. If someone had intervened in my life, maybe it would have turned out very differently. But there was no intervention. Because of this, I have stood in the gap for all the hurting young people out there who felt they had no one. Having suffered from extreme loneliness most of my life, I know what it is like when there is one person who is prepared to stand up for you and who cares for you. It can literally save someone's life.

Because I had seen the most broken of broken, and walked alongside those whom society rejects, I found a desire for everyone to feel accepted and loved. My husband and I founded a program for the homeless and disadvantaged on the Sunshine Coast called Streetlight. This organisation showed people that they were valuable and loved, despite where they found themselves in life. Many said that because of the love we showed them without judgement, and our ability to accept them right where they were at, it helped to transform their lives. After all, we are not defined by our past but merely shaped by it.

In January 2017, after experiencing a long period of grief from losing both of my parents and other family members, as well as watching as my husband battled with chronic illness and a breakdown, I came to a point where I felt utterly defeated. I knew this feeling from before, but this time it was worse than ever. I barely felt like I could go on. All HOPE seemed lost. I felt all alone. Having become the person others went to for refuge and help, I found myself in a dark tunnel barely able to see the light. I have heard the comment all too often, "Kerrie, you look like you have it all together." Well, I want to tell the world right now: everyone needs encouragement. Never presume someone is just okay. Often, it's the people you would least expect who can be suffering internally the most.

After a couple of months of almost isolation from the outside world and spending much of my time alone with one whom I did find solace in - God - I slowly started to heal the pain in my life. I forced myself to attend a women's conference. There was a defining moment that day as I saw three people up on stage. One was Sunshine Coast's greatly loved chef Matt Golinski, who five years ago had tragically lost his family in a fire. He was up doing what he loved; a cooking demonstration and bringing joy to others. He had a purpose that had carried him through his pain. The other two people who spoke that day included a man who had experienced absolute atrocities as a child and had gone on to help others find freedom, and a lady who had been through immense grief and faced the hardest of challenges after losing her husband and father. She had also been seriously injured in an accident. These people were sharing their stories of how they had overcome adversity and found their purpose.

I started thinking about all the things I had been through and the many things I had overcome in my life and realised that if these brave people could stand up on that stage after all they have been through and go on to live their life with purpose, I could also. Right there in that room, something powerful happened inside me. I had the 'lightbulb moment' and I was determined that I would not lie down any longer, but I would rise up and live out my purpose in the world around me and change as many lives as I possibly could. I knew that I had not been through the pain in my life for nothing. I was given the inspiration that day to go on and to inspire and bring HOPE to those in the world around me. Many of the clients I counselled often expressed that I was the only person they felt they could talk to. Many lived in desperate circumstances, experienced deep loneliness and a very real sense of shame for the situations they found themselves in. Many ended up in drug addiction and had done things and crossed moral boundaries that they never thought they would.

Coming back from that is so hard because they literally had lost who they were and didn't know how to go forward.

Seeing the need so great in our community, with lack of human connection at its all-time highest, along with a climbing suicide rate, I thought about all the hard times I had come out of and the many people I also knew who had also overcome such adversity in their lives. I knew that if I could create a space where people could come together from all walks of life, no matter what they believed in or what state they were in, I could literally help save thousands of lives at once.

Three months later, in January 2017, I started Stories of HOPE Australia. With the need so great and only so many hours in the day, I wanted to start something that could literally reach the masses. Stories of HOPE carries a no religious, political or business agenda policy, because I didn't want any barriers at all. Even though I myself have my own spiritual beliefs, I hold this all-inclusive policy so the only agenda ever allowed is simply to give and receive HOPE. For such a time as this, the walls come down and genuine connection takes place. People feel accepted and are gathered together for the common good as well as for one another.

There comes a time in everyone's life when they will need to hear a story of HOPE. That story could be the very thing that goes on to show them their purpose, to cause them to know that they are not alone in their time of suffering and that there are others who have gone before them and come out the other side. To know this could literally save their lives, because then they may not give up. They will keep going. People need to know that their life is worth living. That they were born for a greater purpose. That today is the first day of the rest of their life and despite what has been, the rest of their life can be much greater than the past. Grace

> There comes a time in everyone's life when they will need to hear a story of HOPE.

means that we all deserve a second chance. We all need HOPE. It is my desire that nobody in this world does life alone. Together really is better. Ultimately faith, HOPE and love are the things that have the greatest power to change lives. Faith and HOPE for a greater tomorrow and love for one another.

www.empowerlifesolutions.com.au
https://www.facebook.com/StoriesofHOPEAustralia/

Mark John Castro

From Heartache to Hero: A grieving father finds purpose in teaching disadvantaged kids boxing

OUR FIRST CONNECTION

It was New Year's Eve, 2016, and I was looking at notifications posted on our local Sunshine Coast Community Facebook page. It was there I saw a heartfelt message which said this: "I am lonely and have just moved from Sydney and have no family or friends here. Is anyone free to hang out so I don't have to do New Year's Eve alone?" My heart broke for this young guy. I was away in Sydney but knew of an event which was on, so I told him about it. He went along. About four months later, he commented on one of my Stories of HOPE event ads saying he had a story to tell. When I responded back with a message, he was surprised to find out that I was the same lady who had answered his ad and helped him that New Year's Eve. We had a very long chat on the phone and he shared all of the very hard times he had experienced in his life and excitedly told me everything had really turned around since our first connection. I was so inspired, I asked him to speak at my event. Here is his moving story in his own words...

What happens to us in our childhood, whether good or bad, leaves an imprint on our mind and in our heart and soul that is hard to erase. In my case, the imprint left was one of brokenness, abandonment, violence and dysfunction.

I was born and grew up in the Philippines. I have one older sister and we came from a broken family. *That's life growing up in a third world country,* or so I thought. I just accepted it as normal, I guess, as I had never known any different back then.

Instead of being smacked for doing the wrong thing, I was beaten with belts, sticks and planks of wood until they broke over my arms and legs. Physical pain wasn't all I endured. This kind of treatment was soul crushing. Especially for a twelve-year-old boy. I never understood why I fought so much with other kids or never had the right to ever explain myself.

The treatment I had suffered at the hands of my aunty had obviously taken its toll and caused me to hyperventilate, suffer with anxiety, have anger outbursts, and at times cry uncontrollably. It wasn't until I started to experience such negative emotions that I realised something wasn't right.

One day, when I was just three years of age, my mother kicked my father out of our family home after I told my mum about the lady I knew instinctively he was having an affair with. I remember those first three years of my life vividly. I witnessed the heartbreak and hardship my mother went through living in an abusive relationship at the hands of my father.

I have plenty of cousins and many great-aunties and -uncles. However, after many years of my mum struggling financially to provide for us, she eventually went overseas to work, leaving us in the care of one aunty and uncle. They were meant to look after us, or so I thought. The ages of twelve to fifteen were hell for me. That is when the abuse at the hands of my aunty started. My mother was the most hardworking, devoted, caring and loving mother. While she was away working overseas to raise enough money to care for us from a distance, I was being emotionally and physically abused back in the Philippines. This was something my mum would not find out about until many years later.

When I was fifteen, my life took a real turn in a positive direction. My mum remarried a caring and amazing man who became my stepdad. I finally had a man in my life who I knew would care for me and my family. Someone who could be a role model and rescue us from difficult times, someone whom I could look up to as an example of the real way a father should treat his family.

It was 1997 when he brought us over to Australia to live with him and my stepsister. Our wonderful new life in the land of Oz had just begun. I could finally leave the devastation of the past behind me and look forward to great times and a new future. Everything seemed perfect. Too perfect, and suddenly so easy. But on the other hand, easy was something I was in no way accustomed to. I found it hard to adjust.

For the first time in our lives, we didn't have to worry about things many people take for granted, like everyday essentials such as food, bills and the cost of education. This was so foreign to me to not have to struggle and for some strange reason, I started to lose motivation and miss my old home town in the Philippines and the company of my extended family. I finally finished my studies and then decided to move out of home.

Moving out and growing up wasn't easy, especially in a different country with a different culture and lifestyle. Not having my Philippino relatives and friends around for support and guidance like I used to forced me to have to learn things the hard way. I ended up hanging out with the wrong crowd. I followed western society's main definition of happiness, which to me at the time, was partying and getting drunk. The whole time, deep inside, I was looking for what I felt had been missing my whole life. I was craving a deep sense of love, family and a sense

> I was looking for what I felt had been missing my whole life.

of belonging. I knew I was looking for something, but I didn't know for sure what it was I was looking for. I felt lost!

Then I met my first girlfriend. Maybe this relationship would fill the void inside and be the answer to my heart's desires? But like every young relationship, being immature and inexperienced, it broke down, which led me to move to Sydney in 2001. I kept on in my old ways of partying, thinking I would find fulfilment and happiness down that path.

By 2003, I had everything I had ever wanted. Two well-paying jobs in Sydney whilst living in the beautiful suburb of Mosman on the city's north shore and the woman of my dreams. My girlfriend was beautiful, caring and loving. Then in 2005, my girlfriend became pregnant and we had a baby on the way. Everything seemed so perfect but that all changed the fateful day I received a call from her parents while I was at work, telling me that my baby would be arriving way earlier than expected and that my girlfriend was in hospital in early labour.

I rushed to get to the hospital so I could be there to see our little girl being born, but suddenly something was very wrong and there were major complications. This was something I never saw coming in a million years. We were told that our baby was being born prematurely and that there was a very real risk that our baby could have brain damage. As a result, we were told by the doctors that we would have to make the heart-breaking decision about whether or not they should go ahead and revive our baby if her eyes weren't open when she was born.

Our baby was born and died that same day. We named her Mercedez.

> We came home to a total void of emptiness and sadness.

Nothing could have prepared us for the difficult days ahead as not only did we struggle to deal with our grief, but we also had to organise a funeral to bury our precious daughter. Instead of the excitement of bringing our new baby home, we came home to a total void of emptiness and sadness.

A few months down the track, we decided to move to the Gold Coast so we could attempt to recover from the death of our child and start over. I didn't know how to cope with what had happened and started to retreat. I became self-centred and looking back now, felt like I was the worst partner as all I thought about was my own dreams and happiness. I asked my girlfriend if we could try again for another child, not realising that she wasn't ready or really understanding how deeply she was grieving and the effect it'd all had on her.

It wasn't long before we decided to move back to Sydney so she could be much closer to her family and so that she could have a better chance of finding a job. I guess we were both trying to cope with the grief the best way we could and lost sight of each other's needs. My main focus became my job and I stopped taking care of our relationship. I was going through hell because I loved her so much but simply didn't know how to show her. I was so lost and ended up losing her, the love of my life.

I was so depressed and heartbroken. She moved out and I was living by myself with our pet cat. I eventually found another place to live. Around the same time, my best friend Jeffrey died in his sleep at his home on the Gold Coast. I was experiencing the most immense grief. Not only had I lost my daughter, but my partner and now my best friend. My grief and pain were unbearable, and I just longed for a family of my own.

I met another girl thinking that together we could fulfil my dream, but that relationship wasn't to be and quickly fell apart also. Eventually I moved closer to my friends and family. Just as I had started to heal emotionally and feel like my life was starting to come back to some semblance of normal, my grandmother, who was still in the Philippines, died suddenly.

It was in that moment that all the pain of the past few years came back like a tsunami, triggering memories of everything bad that ever happened to me. I felt totally hopeless and really thought life was so unfair. I had been brought up as a devout Catholic and had always had such a strong faith in God, but after going through so much trauma, I totally lost my faith and decided that I would not believe in God anymore like I used to.

My life became totally out of control. I started drinking and gambling a lot as a way of escaping the pain and went out partying almost every night. I believed the false sense that I was happy again. I attempted to totally blot out all reality. I dated girls who either drank too much or smoked weed every day. I no longer had any integrity, meaning or purpose to my life. I didn't value my friends or make time for them anymore. I was making all the wrong decisions for myself. My life was going nowhere. I was looking for the right girl in the wrong places. I was on a very fast downhill slide. I was searching to have the deep void in my life filled, but filling it with all the wrong things, which started to get me into a lot of trouble.

> When we hit rock bottom there is only one way to go if we want to live.

Having become somewhat suicidal I eventually started to question my existence. I had hit rock bottom. When we hit rock bottom there is only one way to go if we want to live, and that is up. I became so motivated by the pain in my life to change things and find HOPE that I started seriously looking at and avoiding all the toxic behaviours and negative people in my life.

Somehow, I managed to reconnect with my best friend Elijah, who helped me look at the direction my life had been going, and he motivated me to ask myself the hard questions. I started to look at and examine my actions and look at how they had impacted and affected everyone and everything around me. I started to take responsibility for my actions, and admit my wrongdoings, asking for forgiveness from those whom I had hurt along the way while I was selfish and immature. I slowed down on partying and drinking and made a genuine attempt to repair the damage in my life.

One of the best decisions I made was to join a Muay Thai gym to help me focus and control my emotions. I managed to have four amateur fights with one of the best Muay Thai gyms in Australia – Boonchu - under Angie and John Wayne Parr. I learnt a lot

> One of the best decisions I made was to join a Muay Thai gym.

and they inspired me to believe that each and every day I could be something so much better than before. I learnt how to have discipline and started to prioritise what was important in my life. That was one big learning curve.

I still dreamt of finding love one day and starting a family. Every time I managed to meet someone, that was always the intention at the forefront of my mind. I was trying to force life rather than letting it come to me naturally and when the time is right.

The more I learnt, the more I discovered how much I did not really know. I was slowly growing each day, though still making many mistakes along the way. The difference was that I was now open to learning new things. Some lessons are harder to learn or accept than others. It had been a very lonely journey because I hardly had any family here in Australia and even though I was getting my life back on track, I was still battling so much emotionally while also trying to survive financially.

Finally, I had a breakthrough … or so I thought. I had landed what seemed like an amazing job on the Gold Coast as a butler and I was living in an infamous Surfers Paradise building. Life seemed amazing, but behind the scenes all was not what it seemed for long. I had been blindsided and was caught up in the middle of a world I hated. One where partying, corruption and drug use were rampant and one where I was voiceless and felt unable to speak up for myself and what I now believed in. I knew in my heart of hearts it was just a matter of time and the new environment I found myself living in would not end well. All my fears became a reality when one day, my friend jumped out of the building to his death. After this, I immediately made my getaway from this job and the seedy environment and moved as far away as I could, back to Sydney.

Even though I had landed a great job which paid great money with a New South Wales transport company, my deep desire to have a family of my own and another baby led me into another relationship that was destined for destruction. This time, I reconnected with an ex-girlfriend who smoked weed every day, something I greatly detested. We were in a long-distance relationship and she lived in Coolum on the Sunshine Coast. Believing she loved me and that she would change and give up her partying ways for me, led me like a gypsy to be enticed to leave the bright lights of Sydney behind and try and start over, yet again.

I accepted a casual position working fewer hours on the Sunshine Coast. Two months was all it took for me to realise I had settled for less than what I deserved. This time, I was voiceless. My self-esteem was at an all-time low and I felt totally defeated, like I had nothing left to give. My ex-girlfriend was a good person, but our beliefs regarding alcohol and substance abuse were on opposite ends of the spectrum and I couldn't live in that environment for another day longer.

As a last attempt, when I did try and voice my thoughts, she took extreme offence and turned it around on me, accusing me of attacking her personally. She even told me I was mentally unstable and that I needed to go and seek professional help. She made me believe that I was the problem. Then she broke up with me, leaving me in a state of self-doubt and feeling totally rejected, betrayed, used, all alone, and abandoned knowing no one in this new town I had moved to. I felt totally defeated, like I had nothing left and everything that had once been important to me didn't matter anymore. I had thrown in the towel.

Not in my right mind, I decided to give all my things of value to her. I left her my Bankcard for her to still deduct my share of rent and use whatever money was left to help her, making sure I had at least enough money to feed myself. I was hurt, depressed and totally alone. That day, I became homeless. I didn't want to let any of my friends or family know I was living in the park and had hoped that this girl, the one person I thought would stop or prevent me from putting myself in that position, really loved me. But she chose alcohol and weed over me. I was the furthest thing from her mind. It sent me a very loud message that I was totally worthless.

I didn't know becoming homeless could happen so easily and sometimes it happens because people just give up on life. I was beyond caring what anyone else thought about me anymore. Life was now at the lowest point it had ever been. I had totally hit rock bottom. Homelessness was something I never imagined could happen to someone like me, who had always worked so hard to support myself and those I loved. I slept on the park bench right in front of the beach. Mosquitos bit my hands and face if I didn't cover them while I slept at night. I had to find shelter when it started to rain. I couldn't cook a fresh meal. But despite all the sadness I felt, I had this deep sense that somewhere, somehow, there were people out there who did love me, including people I didn't know and was yet to meet.

> Homelessness was something I never imagined could happen to someone like me.

I kept telling myself repeatedly that I would never be defeated. Being alone with my thoughts gave me the ability to start processing the way I had been thinking, and I started to accept that pain is part of life. I began to realise that life is like a roller coaster: it has its ups and its downs, along with its twists and turns and you could be thrown in all directions at once. It was uncomfortable, but it just made me push myself. Fuelled by my hunger and not having enough to eat because my ex was accessing most of my money, I started training and teaching people boxing and Muay Thai in the park to earn some extra cash for food. I also started giving free lessons to families that couldn't afford to pay or take their children to a martial arts school.

It made me realise that there are people out there who are also in worse situations than I was, and that I had all this love inside me that I should be giving away freely now, rather than saving it up for the future or someone that may not accept, deserve, appreciate or understand it. I had a revelation that you can give to others, unconditionally, for service as a human being and that love is infinite. The more you let it flow and the more you give, the more you can receive. I learnt that bad experiences don't need to stay as a negative but can be turned into a positive. Good things can come from the hard times and I began to realise there is a reason for everything. It is all about how we perceive it.

Deep down, I was still me on the inside. Even though I had been deeply hurt by people, I remained open without putting a guard around myself for protection. One day I dared to take a chance at connection again and in the process, I met (Stories of HOPE founder) Kerrie after posting an ad on the Sunshine Coast Community board on New Year's Eve in 2016. My ad said this: *I am away from home, friends and family and I honestly don't want to do New Year's Eve alone. Is there anyone out there who could spend it with me*?

Kerrie responded and told me that even though she was away, she knew of a church gathering in Maroochydore where there were some really kind young people. I had many other amazing, helpful, friendly and compassionate people reach out to me that day. I went along to the gathering and afterwards got invited to Mudjimba to celebrate New Year's Eve by the beach with them. On my way home that night, I had one of the best things ever happen to me. After riding the twenty-eight kilometres to get to the church on my push bike, I had to ride back to Mudjimba and stopped by a Thai restaurant to buy some dinner. Using my phone to pay for it, it was rejected. The $20 I had left in there was all gone and the ex-girlfriend still had my actual credit card. I was unaware that was all I had left. But the couple who owned the restaurant gave me the food for free.

I didn't know how to thank them or even say it in words. I left with the food as they closed the shop and sat in the park all by myself crying uncontrollably. I was so happy that people like them still existed. I felt loved and cared for as a person. I had tears of joy streaming down my face. I looked at my food as a gift of love from strangers who never knew me but didn't hesitate to care for me. It just made me even more determined to give and help others in every way I could from this point forward. I wanted to share my life experiences with others, so it could save them from being depressed, hopeless and suicidal like I had been. I wanted to be able to give HOPE to people to realise that love can heal and be the answer to almost any question in life. How it can give us meaning and purpose and how it makes us feel significant.

Today I'm still learning and growing. I now know for sure that every obstacle you beat is a step forward and life goes on. There are things that are way beyond your control, but despite what we are going through, we can all touch other people's lives and make a difference. I now teach boxing and Muay Thai kickboxing at Mojo 365 and I still offer free training for those who can't afford it. I value time more than ever before and choose carefully who I spend it on. I measure everything with time, not with numbers. I now have a place to stay and I am comfortable.

I am planning to study again this year to be qualified in community services or some sort of life coaching course, so I can continue helping others. I am happier than ever, I have more time for myself, for nature, cooking healthy meals and sometimes reading. I am making more friends and meeting wonderful people who also teach me new things to improve myself and other people around me. I am more grateful and have decided to stay where I am instead of running away again. I am still scared of starting over again and I have an all-or-nothing attitude when it comes to my dreams. But something I am determined to continue doing today is daring to dream again because I still love life and everything that it brings.

www.facebook.com/deepmeaningfulconversations/
deepmeaningfulconversations369@gmail.com

Leonie Fay Mulgrew

An Unbreakable Spirit: The transformation from child abuse victim to radiant survivor

OUR FIRST CONNECTION

I went to a local church service one morning on the Sunshine Coast and at the end, turned around to the row behind and saw that my lovely friend Michelle had brought her friend Leonie along for a first-time visit. She had a rare beauty and radiance. She had just found HOPE right there that day, in the midst of a battle with throat cancer. Leonie was not a stranger to hard times though. She had endured and weathered the fiercest and ugliest circumstances of life throughout her childhood as a victim of physical and sexual abuse and neglect. But her past didn't win and she had risen up out of the ashes to find a fulfilling career working as a beauty therapist so she could help other women to feel beautiful and learn how to value themselves. She is the most loving wife and mum, encourager and friend anyone could wish for. Leonie possesses such a contagious zest for life, spreading happiness wherever she goes. This truly shone through when she took to the Stories of HOPE stage to share her story, which she also recounts here...

As I write this, I am fifty-eight years old and would have to say I am a walking miracle, as I never thought I would live through the horrors of my childhood. I also never thought I would see the carefree days of adolescence afforded to so many others, experience life the way others do, or know the love of a caring husband, let alone the blessing of raising three amazing children. This I have been granted and so much more. The joy of the present has far outweighed the pain of the past, if that is even at all possible.

My life started in the midst of horrific dysfunction. I am the youngest from my mother's first marriage. She had three children to my father. She married him when she was only sixteen years old and left him when she was twenty-one. I was still only a baby at that time, six months old to be exact. My mum came from a very dysfunctional family herself and from what I can gather, she was the victim of an extremely mental, physical and sexually abusive environment.

When she left my father, she also left my older brother and sister behind with him but decided to take me. My mum met another man and soon after had a baby with him, who would be my cherished little sister Kim. Not long after that, the new relationship failed and being unable to care for Kim and me, my mother had us placed together in a children's home in Rockhampton. My mum then began to travel up north where she found a job with a lovely man called Bruce, who later became my adored stepdad. Little did I know I would not get to spend much time with him.

Bruce's wife had left him with five children and so my mum became his nanny and was now essentially the mum of nine children, although at the time not caring for any of her biological children. When she had been with him a while, she came and got Kim and me out of the home and we went to live with them. I was four and Kim was two. She then fell pregnant with my younger sister Maxine. Just before Maxine was born, the saddest tragedy occurred. My beautiful little sister and best friend on this earth died. Her appendix burst. Kim was two-and-a-half. This absolutely devastated my mum and she plummeted downward into a world of alcohol and barbiturate abuse. She went on to have another three children with my stepdad. He was a truck driver and away a lot, so was oblivious to the chaos and devastation of what was happening at home.

My mum would send us to school with no lunch and no shoes. She would drink a lot and have other men visit when he wasn't there. She used to say she thought I reminded her of my biological father and that she wished I would have died instead of Kim. These words were so hurtful and broke my little heart. On top of this I bore the brunt of my mother's behaviour and because my stepbrothers and sisters didn't like my mum, they took it out on me. My life was about to take a devastating turn for the worse when my mum broke up with my stepdad when I was eleven. She left town with a younger man and took myself and my younger brothers and sisters with her to start a new life, also leaving my stepbrothers and stepsisters behind, who were old enough and had already left home.

This new man in my mother's life started making sexual advances towards me. I was terrified, and I told my mum, but sadly she didn't believe me and then she threatened to drop me off to live with my biological father. She came good on her threat, but prior to my arrival there, I soon learnt that

> I was terrified, and I told my mum, but sadly she didn't believe me.

he had a new wife and three children with her. Two girls and one boy. Just before I moved in, the boy, my half-brother, had drowned. He was only nine years old. My real father was basically a stranger to me after all these years. At first, he seemed to treat me well and appeared to be nice in the beginning, but that was short-lived. Before long, it started.

He would come into my room at night and climb into my bed, which was in a room I shared with my two younger sisters. He started out fondling and kissing me and touching me where he should not and I felt dirty and ashamed and could not understand how no one else in the house didn't know he was in my bed. Was anyone going to protect me? This terrifying abuse went on for nine long months until one day when l went to school and found the courage to tell my friend what had been happening to me at home.

My father was not only sexually abusive but abusive in many other ways and up until that point, I felt totally trapped and alone in such a hopeless situation. One morning soon after, I arrived at school and the police were there waiting for me with my friend and his mum. I will be forever so thankful and grateful to him for reporting the abuse and putting an end to this horrendous form of torment in my life.

They sent me back home to my mum who was by this time back with my stepdad. I was so happy to see them together again and my HOPE for better days ahead had risen, even though things had not changed with my mum. She still refused to believe the truth about what my biological father had done to me and started calling me a liar. She almost killed me with her many destructive words and continually put me down, calling me useless over and over again. That is when the many floggings started at her hands. I had to get away. I couldn't stand the continual abuse anymore and started to run away at any given opportunity. I didn't know where I was going, but anywhere was better than living in the hell I had been for my short few years of being alive.

> I couldn't have had any idea what horror awaited me on the other side.

The second last time I ran away, the twelfth time to be exact, would be a very fateful decision. I couldn't have had any idea what horror awaited me on the other side of that escapade just a few days later.

I was only eleven years old and I wanted out so badly that I hitchhiked from Shepparton in Victoria to

Inglewood in Queensland, literally thousands of kilometres. A truck driver had picked me up and as we roared along the outback dirt roads in the middle of nowhere, I was totally oblivious to the horror that was about to unfold. I can't remember anything much about that day, other than the accident and what happened after. I can remember the feeling of the truck as it started rolling and then tucking my head into my lap and putting my left arm up to shield my face from the brute force. As a result, my arm took the full brunt of the impact as acid burned right through my clothes and onto my skin.

I remember waking up in the back of a police car as I was being rushed to Warwick Base Hospital. All my clothes had been burnt right off my little body and I was being covered by the police officer's shirt. When the truck crashed, it was out the back of nowhere and police had been close by on road patrol. They made a decision that it would be quicker to take me to hospital in the police car as it would take too long for an ambulance to arrive and I wouldn't have survived because my injuries were so severe. I had terrible burns to a large percentage of my body and was in extreme shock and deteriorating quickly. I ended up being in hospital for six weeks and had to endure six months of treatment for the burns to my body. Nobody turned up at the hospital to support me except my two step sisters, Margaret and Lyn.

After I left the hospital, I was again returned to my mother in Victoria. But I ran away again. This time would be the last time. My mum's abuse, alcohol and substance intake had reached a new level and my stepdad was never around. After running the last time, I was picked up by the police for being exposed to moral danger. How shocking to think that I, just a child, was charged with moral danger. That is just the unthinkable. A female police officer took pity on me and rather than have me spend the night in jail while they worked out what to do with me, she took me to her house. She was like an angel sent right at the time

> I was now homeless at the age of twelve.

when I needed someone the most! I was now homeless at the age of twelve with nothing but the clothes on my back. I had no belongings, and no place to call my home.

The court decided to place me in Winberra, which was like a detention centre for girls. I was there for three months before going back to court to see if my mother would take me back. As I waited at court that day for my mum, for anyone, nobody came. I was totally alone in this world. Because nobody turned up to claim me, I was then sent to Winlaton Girls' Training Centre and made a ward of the state. I was remanded for another three months and then put in a state prison for girls under the age of eighteen.

I reached out for my mum to take me back because the hell of home had to be better than the hell of being a child in prison, but all she could say to me was, "You made your bed, you lie in it." She refused to take me back. My fate was to have to stay there until I was eighteen, something I couldn't bear the thought of. I may have been young in age, but I had learnt to grow up very fast. I had to in order to survive. In a last, desperate attempt, I had the insight to write to a local priest and asked if he could help me and find me somewhere to live.

This was a decision that would ultimately turn my life around for good. He put me in touch with St Margaret's Training Centre in Oakley, which was run by the Good Shepherd Nuns. The love the nuns showed me really built my confidence and helped me through so much. I was there for five years in total and was fostered out every Christmas. This was a place where, for the first time in my life, I was shown love and care. I was finally nurtured in a fabulous caring environment where I was clothed, fed, and taught. All the things that should, in a perfect world, be the right of any child. But in my world, they hadn't. These were things I had to fight for. Finally, I had HOPE.

> I was finally nurtured in a fabulous caring environment.

At sixteen years of age, I left the only real home I had ever known and started a hairdressing apprenticeship. My boss was very caring. Not only did I have a job, but I also had a place to call home. I boarded with her for six months until I moved back to Queensland. There, I met a boy and lived with him for four years whilst working as a hairdresser and beauty therapist in Brisbane. I graduated from South Bank TAFE in 1974. It was such a huge achievement for me despite my rough start to life. But the relationship finished, as I realised having never had a real childhood, I was just too young to settle down and I needed to explore life for the first time ever. My life was really on track and then the only dad I had ever really known and loved died suddenly at the age of fifty-six of a heart attack. I was absolutely devastated. I packed up and went and lived in Hawaii for eighteen months, continuing my work in hairdressing by day and worked in a bar by night.

Because of my horrific upbringing, I had always declared that I would never have children, but my whole world changed in a heartbeat when I fell pregnant with my first baby at the age of twenty-four. For the first time in my life I felt like I belonged to someone, and that they belonged to me. Another being who could love me back the way I loved them. It was the best feeling ever and one that is indescribable. Then only two weeks after my beautiful little Tihanna was born, I met the love of my life Shane while out on a girls' night. I have always said that Shane fell in love with Tihanna before he fell in love with me. Having Tihanna and meeting Shane totally transformed my life and birthed my desire to have more children. Over those next six years I was blessed with two more beautiful children. Kirsten three years later, and three years after that, Trent.

My family and friends have given me more joy than I could have ever imagined. I have had the kind of life that I only ever dreamed would be possible. I have worked in the beauty industry ever since and had the opportunity to meet and connect with people from all walks of life who have been through all kinds of things. I love making people feel good about themselves and to be able to have a job that does just that is absolutely amazing. The experiences I endured in my own childhood, which were tragic and could have easily destroyed me, only served as a resolve to be an even greater wife and mum to my own children than the role model I had. I don't condone what my parents did to me, but I have been able to forgive them. No child should ever have to go through the kind of inhumane things that I experienced at their hands, but to be able to move forward and be the best I could be, I had to forgive.

> In order to truly forgive, we need to be patient with ourselves.

In order to truly forgive, we need to be patient with ourselves and we need to realise that we all heal differently, but we don't have to be a product of our environment, and today I am living proof of that fact. Three years ago, I was diagnosed with throat cancer, something I was healed from and am now free of. I am a born survivor! know that the resilience I learnt in my early years was a great contributor to the victory I have over any difficulty that has come my way. All in all, I must say that despite my past, I have a real zest for living and I feel blessed and have extreme joy for the wonderful life I am living today.

www.facebook.com/leoniemulgrew

Dave Larkin

Home is Where the Heart is: Homelessness doesn't discriminate

OUR FIRST CONNECTION

I had never liked school camps, and this was my first camp since school days. It seemed rather strange, especially as I was now an adult, but nevertheless it was a requirement for my new job. It wasn't just any camp, we were being trained to be chaplains. I was feeling quite isolated and in unfamiliar territory when, out of the corner of my eye at the large dining table, I saw a guy with a red cap. Red was one of my favourite colours and I instantly knew I had found someone like me who was out of the box. Within minutes I felt like I had found my twin. We had been through many of the same circumstances in life that had led us to want to work in schools to help children at risk and prevent them from ending up where we did. Not only that, we wanted to shine a light for others and show them that despite the past, a great future is possible. I had absolutely no idea at the time that Dave was going through one of the hardest chapters in his life, but I was soon to find out the true extent of the journey and the resilience of this humble guy who won the Sunshine Coast 2016 Citizen of the Year award. This is Dave's story...

I remember the day well when my wife and I found out that we were pregnant with our fifth child. We were excited, elated, shocked and a little dismayed as we looked at our four other children, who were huddled in the tent where we had been living in our friend's backyard. This was the first time of many, where we would find ourselves homeless on the Sunshine Coast. The timing couldn't have been more difficult, but where HOPE was concerned, this little man growing in my wife's belly would be such a joy to us all in such a difficult season of cyclical homelessness.

Knocking on the door of real estate agents nine months later, desperately trying to find accommodation with a heavily pregnant wife, I wondered if this was how Mary and Joseph felt when continuously hearing the words, "sorry, no room for you". At least we didn't have to travel by donkey! Finally, we were forced to settle on a holiday rental at Golden Beach, as we just couldn't get accepted for a permanent rental no matter how hard I tried and pleaded. And here our son was born, home-birthed in a temporary dwelling. Needless to say, I suffered immense anxiety as the family provider and I felt extreme shame as an Australian man who, even though working hard for a carrying company, just couldn't provide the permanent security of long-term accommodation.

We moved many times between holiday rentals and what ended up unfortunately being different short-term permanent rentals, but never for the reason that we didn't pay our rent on time. In fact, we always made this top priority and we continually left places in better condition than when we first arrived. Landlords would want to either renovate, sell, put the price up or move back in, which sadly always saw us on the move again after a short period of time. The Sunshine Coast housing boom had blessed many and left others in the turbulent waters, tossed to and fro at the mercy of the very competitive arena, trying to secure a permanent rental at an affordable price.

Having five children and a much-loved family pet meant that our applications were usually put to the side as an unlikely, or a plain "no chance". I dreaded going to house inspections with so many other families so desperate for housing also. I would turn up to some places and choose not to even go in due to the amount of people applying. The cycle of getting your hopes up, filling in endless amounts of applications only to hear another, "sorry, you didn't get the house", became very tiring and demoralising. We learned a lot about ourselves, our family and who our true friends were during those hard years.

We did, however, have the pleasure during those difficult times of living in some pretty unique houses and units. A lot of them were either too small or very old. But some of those places were amazing, like the old Queenslander that we stayed in for a time in the middle of town or the old farmhouse on thirty-three acres where the kids and the dog could run around and go crazy to their hearts content! We lived with friends and an employer once, either in tents or in their homes, which was just so humbling and beautiful. But there were times when we felt exposed, humiliated and trapped.

Eventually we decided that enough was enough. We were sick of the cycle and we packed our belongings into storage, bought a trailer and camping gear and travelled Australia for nine months in our $500 aptly-named Nissan Nomad. We were searching for a new perspective and we sure got one, bigger and better than my fears expected. When you pack a family of seven into a car and a tent for nine months, you are soon going to find out who you really are! Fun times, adventure and lots of precious moments of reading books to the kids are some of my best memories during that time. The worst are the arguments, the fears and the uncertainty of the future, my escapism through alcohol and the endless arguments and denial I had going on in my head regarding returning home to the Sunshine Coast. I had determined in my heart and in my mind, that there was nothing left for me 'back there' and that only shame and humiliation would be my inheritance in that place.

In my dreams and in my magical thinking during the final stages of our trip in Tasmania, I desperately wanted to stay there and build what I thought would be a much better life. But in reality, there was no way my wife and kids would have wanted to stay there. Not to mention how darn cold it was. The Sunshine Coast was still and would always be home to them in their hearts and in their souls.

One night, whilst camping in Bridport, Northern Tasmania, I was contemplating life on the end of a cask of port, when I finally gave in and had a spiritual moment. Whilst it wasn't the audible voice of God that boomed these things out loud, or a flashy looking sparkly angel, I knew quietly in my heart that I had a peace beyond my own understanding. I was going to take my family home and I had a great desire to become a school-based chaplain. I certainly had come out the other side of many things in my own childhood and teen years and had a real desire to make a difference in the lives of kids going through hard times. Of course, going back to the place where I had experienced many difficulties and negative situations would certainly not be easy. Mindsets and expectations need to have paradigm shifts sometimes. Some don't shift as easily as we had shifted house.

> Mindsets and expectations need to have paradigm shifts sometimes.

We did have an early breakthrough on the Sunshine Coast, much to my surprise. I walked into the first real estate agent and told them of our situation and within a day, we had a new permanent rental! I felt like the red carpet had been rolled out, shouting, "Welcome home Larkin Family!" It wasn't our ideal house, but we were comfortable and finally it felt like some semblance of a home. After breaking my ankle, I ceased work as a car detailer and finally decided to embark on my journey to become a chaplain. Now you may be thinking that working for God in a school would get you brownie points and that our homeless situation would be done and dusted, but unfortunately that wasn't the case.

As had happened many times before, the landlord wanted to sell and once again we ended up moving into another larger rental that we couldn't really afford. This time we took in boarders to help out with the rent and ended up having a falling out with them, which again left us with nowhere to go but back into a friend's house and share accommodation again. This became an uncomfortable situation and we moved in with a family. This saw seven of us sharing two bedrooms and an open lounge room with a small kitchenette. Needless to say, I was struggling and that old paradigm was looking like a blinding truth that things were never going to change and that this would be our reality forever. *Here we go again*, went around and around aimlessly in my head.

During this time, I had been appointed as a school chaplain and the real breakthrough in my paradigm shift finally came when we first arrived at another house after getting the news that we had been approved for this private rental. It was an old farmhouse and just happened to be right near the school where I was the chaplain. The farmhouse was on acreage and was very damp, cramped and out in the middle of nowhere. We had an old outdoor shower in an old water tank and a very small kitchen, but I looked at my family and finally, without any anxiety, said with confidence for the first time, "Guys, it's not the house that makes the home, but the people in it." I said it and I meant it. This old shack that we were in for eight months gave us shelter, warmth and a place to laugh and love each other in.

I will never forget the day we received a huge twelve-seater wooden

> "Guys, it's not the house that makes the home, but the people in it."
> I said it and I meant it.

> I wasn't happy, but more importantly, I knew that my thinking had finally changed.

table that we could barely fit in the dining room and I said to my kids, "One day we will put this table into a big house where we all can fit and enjoy it." Funnily enough, or ironically enough, a couple of weeks later, we found out that we had to move yet again. The landlord had two properties and needed to move back into the old shack. Once again, back to live with family with the two rooms and the kitchenette. I wasn't happy, but more importantly, I knew that my thinking had finally changed. My wife and I worked out that in the nineteen-year period we had been married and lived together, we had moved more than twenty times. The only things that remained stable for us, was my work, school and our love for each other. All of that was about to change in an instant with the help of some very generous and caring friends who knew of our situation.

These amazing friends had bought a large family home just for us to rent. The day I found out, I was on my knees crying in the middle of my friend's shop. It could not have been more perfect for us in every way. Five bedrooms, a large open living area and a backyard for our dog. This poor dog had moved all over the place as we shifted from one dwelling to the next. Not only did they buy a house big enough for us to fit our enormous table and our large family in, but such was their generosity that they rented it out to us at a very affordable price. (Much less than they could have charged us for it). We had never known such stability and eventually as a family, we decided to help share this generosity and stability with others. We became foster carers, having other people's children come to find refuge and love in our home. We stayed for six years in that home, something that we had not experienced as a family ever before. There was, as usual, another twist around the corner in our "Home is Where the Heart is" adventure.

It was Father's Day 2017, the second since my dad had passed away after a horrible time with dementia and illness. I had received an inheritance from him, but we knew that it wasn't quite going to be enough to give us a breakthrough in the property market, especially on my chaplaincy wages. But we were content and forever thankful for our rental, which was given so generously to us to reside in for as long as we required it. Then out of nowhere, an amazing couple that we knew approached my wife and I on that Father's Day morning and told us they wanted to speak to us about something. I thought nothing of it as we had talked about many things together from football to foster care. I will never forget the words that they uttered that day, "We want to help you buy a house".

We were in shock. I didn't know what to say; my mind went numb and my emotions wanted to jump out and go crazy like a bird getting out of a cage and flying freely for the first time. You *what*? They then proceeded to offer us a ridiculously generous amount of money with no motive at all attached, just love and compassion. The very next day, my wife had found our dream home. Everything that we had ever dreamed of in a house had the possibility of becoming a reality. We found an old Queenslander on acreage with heaps of rooms, loads of character and even a swimming pool. We scraped in by the skin of our teeth and made an offer with the generous cash deposit. We only had to nervously wait one day, which seemed like a lifetime, to find out the result of our offer. And you guessed it, the impossible breakthrough for our family came through and had really happened.

Our dream was now a reality! We had finally bought our own home. Not just any old home, but one that finally suited and fitted us all. We are settling in to all the things that homeowners are accustomed to, like doing renovations and maintenance, lawn mowing and

> It really has become our reality, that, home truly has been where the heart is.

pool cleaning. But hey, no complaining here. There is a peace in my heart and mind knowing that our family is a family, no matter where we have been over the years. I can't say it enough, because for us it really has become our reality, that, home truly has been where the heart is.

My story is hopefully one that gives you inspiration and encouragement in knowing that mental breakthroughs, as well as physical breakthroughs, are so liberating when we change our perspective on things. Thankfulness and contentment can only come when we see our situations as glass half-full rather than glass half-empty, as I had for so long. I still have to work on this some days, but that's okay. I am forever grateful to our family and friends who supported us rather than judge us as we went through the ups and downs of our homeless cycles. To our generous friends who shared their homes, bought us a rental and eventually our own home, we will forever remember your sacrificial love, generosity and blessing to us. You all gave us great HOPE.

www.facebook.com/david.larkin.146

Stuart Rawlins

From Top Dog to The Black Dog and Back Again: The story of one of the leading investigators in Australia's biggest murder investigation – the Daniel Morcombe case

OUR FIRST CONNECTION

It was a casual comment as I was finishing up a meeting with a lady I met on LinkedIn. This person said, "Maybe you should try and link up with a guy called Stuart Rawlins. He is a former cop who has a similar interest like you in helping people with mental health issues." Not one to shy away from new opportunities, I sent him a message on LinkedIn and he responded immediately. Stuart is a former Sunshine Coast detective and was one of the leading investigators in Australia's biggest murder investigation – the Daniel Morcombe case. Stuart spoke at my event two months later and has remained a pivotal part of my team ever since. He is my go-to person, the one I bounce everything off and the one I check everything against. Today I call him a friend. He shares my vision and has run alongside me every step of the way with equal passion to help change as many lives as possible in our community and beyond. He is the perfect person, being a former police officer, to help me make decisions on the right people to have involved in my passion. Now an advocate for mental health, Stuart shares his story of how he went from great career highs to the depths of depression. Following a breakdown and suffering the debilitating effects of PTSD, he has now not only found himself, but his true purpose and a new way of living. Here, he tells his story...

Since the mid 2000s, I have battled with a number of mental health conditions as a result of my thirteen-year career, mostly as a detective in the Queensland Police Service. Yes, it would be easy to blame the police service and live a bitter and twisted life thinking about how unfair it was being exposed to a considerable number of traumatic incidents that are simply too gruesome to share in this story. That would be easy. But that is not me and not what I am about. I want to share my story and journey with you to show you that life does go on when you have a mental health condition … or three, and that there is light at the end of that dark tunnel we sometimes find ourselves in.

During this story you will read about some of my challenges and what worked for me to overcome them, but most importantly you will also read about what didn't work for me, in the HOPE that you will not follow that same path. Because trust me, it is always easier to learn from someone else's mistakes and this is your opportunity to learn from mine!

As a twenty-two-year-old, I'd had enough of working indoors all day in my banking job. Having worked for Westpac since finishing high school, it was time for something more interesting, something that would get me outside. So when a friend who had recently graduated as a police officer walked into the Nambour Westpac Bank branch I was working at to say hello while wearing his uniform, I was mesmerized. That was it. I had found my calling, I wanted to become a police officer. Not just any police officer; I wanted to be a detective. I wanted to chase down murderers, rapists and drug dealers. I wanted to deal with the higher end of crime. Even before joining the police service, I had decided I had no interest in writing traffic tickets or doing any of that warm and fuzzy stuff. I wanted to chase the big crooks.

In May of 1997, I was accepted into the police service and my new adventure began. After graduating on December 5, 1997, I was posted to Redcliffe, which is located about fifty-five minutes south of the Sunshine Coast where I was living. Redcliffe was a rough place in 1997 and the perfect location to start my new adventure and dream of becoming a detective. On my first day, I turned up super-early and did everything I had been told to do in the academy. I had booked out all the equipment, the car and had set my bag up ready to meet the senior constable, who was to be my mentor for the next eight weeks. I was so looking forward to a tour of Redcliffe and to hear about what we would be doing over the next eight weeks, but that was not to be.

At that moment a sergeant appeared in the day room and with a deep Pommy accent, he yelled, "Who is on day-shift?" As we put our hands up, he told us that there had been a car accident on the other side of the Bruce Highway and that we had to go to the hospital and collect the trauma team and get them out there as fast as we could. So off we went, lights and sirens blasting up to the hospital, to get the trauma team. With my partner driving it was my job to use the radio and handle the sirens - easier said than done. As I looked down, there was a metal box with black switches on it that went every which way, but no information about what any of them actually did.

Flicking the switches around and trying to speak in the radio was just not working and my mouth was so dry nothing was coming out when I tried to speak, so my partner, who was also driving, took over using the radio. As we drove at speeds of more than twice the signed speed limit I thought to myself how great this is, my first job on my first day was a lights and siren job (Code 2), which in those days meant drive as fast as you possibly can. I was so excited, and I could feel the adrenaline rushing through my body. After we collected the trauma team, I can remember looking over at them while we were driving out to the crash scene and they were being flung from one side of the car to the other from both the speed and the ducking and weaving through the traffic. At that point, they decided it would a good idea to put on their seat belts, but I can tell you that was easier said than done.

As we pulled up at the traffic crash and got out and put on our hats and reflection vests, I can remember thinking to myself,

"I have got this". I had my hat, vest, notebook and was pretty sure I could direct some traffic if I had to. How wrong I was! As I looked up, I could see the car had hit a power pole whilst rounding a bend, it was at that point I was given two young kids to look after. They were about four and six years old and were bleeding from their nose and ears and had no idea what was going on.

My job was to look after the children until another ambulance arrived to treat them as all the attention was on their mum, who was still in the car. As I tried to talk to them, I could see the car behind us being cut open by the fire service. It didn't look good. The kids were continually asking for their mum and it was then I realised I was well out of my depth. All my training at the academy meant nothing. What the hell had I got myself into? I had no answers to give the kids and no idea what I was doing. As I tried my best to keep their attention, I could see behind them their mother being removed from the car. She didn't make it.

To this day I can remember the most intricate details of that moment. The feeling of the hot summer sun beaming down onto me, the sweat running down my back from wearing my vest over the top of my uniform and the thick black polish on the toes of my boots becoming mush from the hot bitumen road. As a twenty-two-year-old, I was lost and I was drowning. I had no idea what I was doing and nothing I had been taught in the previous seven months prepared me for what I had just encountered. What do you say to two young kids continually asking for their mum when you know she has just passed away in the car fifty metres behind them?

As I handed the kids over to the ambulance officers I started to question my decision to become a police officer. With the trauma team refusing to return with us due to our, shall we say *priority*, driving speeds on the way out to the job, we were quickly sent to our next task. Job two for my first day was to be just as interesting as we were to attend and assist the detectives in searching the cars of a number of known drug runners and thieves.

Being as green-as, with a new uniform and the face of an eighteen-year-old, it didn't take long for the seasoned criminals to realise I was a rookie and so the taunts began. That I could handle, but what I found amazing was the ability of two strong men to systematically dismantle the insides of a new Commodore with their bare hands. Finding used syringes shoved down seats, stolen property everywhere and a very odd syrup liquid in a number of large peanut butter containers was an eye-opener (that's another story). So, we were off again, taking one of the offenders back to the watch-house for processing.

With that task sorted it was time for a late lunch ... or so we thought! Job three was a domestic dispute where a drug-crazed man had kicked his drug-crazed pregnant partner in the stomach because she had used the last of the drugs. After getting the ambulance out to check her over and arresting him, we were off back to the watch-house again to lodge him in his accommodation for the night and type up the charges. With my first shift over, I was exhausted both physically and mentally and was looking forward to a more subdued and quieter second day ... if only that was the case!

Unbeknownst to me, the man we had arrested for the domestic incident was found hanging in his cell that afternoon. He had tried to take his life, but was saved in time by the watch-house staff. On day two, my first job involved being formally warned and interviewed on tape by a senior sergeant about the almost-death in custody of the man we had arrested the day prior. This was to determine if we had done anything wrong or in any way contributed to his actions. I can remember thinking my police career was going to be over almost before it began. Thankfully it was not!

For the next couple of years, it was a roller coaster of adrenaline and emotions, high-speed car chases, attending a police shooting, the sad and devastating task of giving death messages, picking up dead bodies and body parts, arresting drug and gun dealers, finding speed labs, going to countless domestic disputes, pub fights and catching armed robbers. As they say, "All good fun." *Not*!

Two-and-a-half-years out of the academy, I managed my first stint relieving in the Criminal Investigation Branch (CIB). I was so stoked as this was getting me closer to my goal joining the CIB and eventually becoming an appointed detective. I will never forget my first job as a relieving Plain Clothes Constable (PCC) in the CIB as it was an armed robbery, where a recently-released schizophrenic mental patient stole a fishing knife from a tackle shop, walked into the adjacent convenience store and held the knife against the neck of a fifteen-year-old boy who was working as the cashier. *A cracker of a job to learn the ropes from a more experienced detective*, I thought. Unfortunately, that wasn't to be the case as there wasn't one working that shift. I was working the shift with a first-year constable who had about two months' service and was completing their rotation through the CIB office.

Interestingly though, that would be a job that would stay with me for a long time and not because I had absolutely no idea what I was doing, but because of the life-changing effects, the robbery had on the fifteen-year-old boy. I stayed in contact with the family for many years and visited their house on numerous occasions to offer support and guidance to the young boy, as he turned into a hardworking man still dealing with the traumatic after-effects of being held at knifepoint by a crazed mental patient.

With three months CIB relieving under my belt, it was back to uniform for a few months before securing a permanent position in the CIB back home on the Sunshine Coast. With just on three years of sworn service out of the academy, I was literally just out of nappies. Most of the detectives I worked with had ten years-plus as a detective in the CIB, with their uniform service on top of that. So began my life of dealing with the higher end of crime, the dangerous offenders, murderers, drug dealers, armed robbers, bikie gangs, covert operations, listening devices, sexual assaults, protracted fraud investigations and a lot of time giving evidence in the courts.

As I worked my way through the three courses/phases of detective training over the next three years, I found myself finishing my last phase course in December 2003. It was a three-week live-in course at Chelmer with only two modules - Drug Trafficking and Homicide. I can still remember watching the news and seeing that a young boy had gone missing on the Sunshine Coast whilst waiting for a bus. Thinking it would all be sorted and he would be found, I didn't take much more notice until one night after coming home I saw on the news that he hadn't been found and a major incident investigation had been kicked off.

Getting back to the Sunshine Coast, I was drafted into the investigation of Daniel Morcombe's disappearance, which would be known as Operation Vista. For the next three years, my home was a major incident room and my routine included daily briefings

> This was an investigation like no other seen before.

and a systematic process that would receive information, assess it, log it and then detail it to a detective to investigate. This was an investigation like no other seen before. At the time of writing this story, it is still the largest investigation ever undertaken by the Queensland Police Service. It was life-consuming and involved dealing with some of society's lowest characters.

Visiting prisons on a weekly basis, talking to paedophiles on the inside and outside of those prison walls was constant; so was the uncovering of other heinous and disgusting sex crimes during our investigations into finding out what happened to Daniel. Seeing first-hand the type and number of depraved sexual predators living amongst us was downright concerning;

learning directly from them how and why they did what they did was life-changing.

My niche was befriending paedophiles and getting them to tell me how they offended, what techniques and strategies they used to gain the trust of a child enough for them to be sexually assaulted. Looking back at it now, I know that I was only able to do this task at that time as I didn't have any kids of my own. With three young children now, I know it is something that I simply could not have done if I'd had kids. With trips around Queensland, New South Wales and Victoria attending prisons to speak to sex offenders, it was apparent that not all sexual offenders fitted the public stereotype. I was amazed at the variance of occupations, community standing and background of some of the offenders we dealt with. One thing that was prominent was that they were all sick individuals with a warped perception of what love meant.

While on the Morcombe case as detectives, we were "non-taskable", which meant that we only worked on the Morcombe case and nothing else. For me, that was until March 2015. On this Sunday afternoon, we were having our lunch in the normal CIB office when one of the team answered a desk phone that was ringing. That phone call resulted in a number of us from the Morcombe case attending a house out in Eudlo and locating two deceased people that had been tortured in the most horrific manner. The person responsible was at the house and he was arrested. He then proceeded to tell me in detail how the two people were murdered whilst also telling me he was going to take my firearm off me and kill me with it.

After working for nineteen hours straight, I managed to get home and have about four hours' sleep before I was off again down to the morgue in Brisbane. I sat and watched the autopsy of both people, one after the other, and took in-depth notes of their injuries. This process took the whole day and is to date the most disturbing autopsies I ever had to watch. My experience was backed up by similar comments made by the pathologist who was performing the autopsies. To top off a massive two days, I stopped off on the way back home and had to give a death message to one of the victim's close relatives. I can remember being so exhausted that I was literally falling asleep behind the wheel of the police car on the Bruce Highway. Realising that I couldn't keep driving, I pulled over and had a half-hour sleep on the side of the highway before finally getting home.

With everything going on, I can remember my wife telling me that after investigating that murder and seeing what I had seen, I was different. I was having flashbacks of the victims and their injuries while I was asleep and also while watching shows on television like NCIS. I was having nightmares where I would run different scenarios through my head: like the offender killing my partners at the house before I could get back and tell them that I had found two bodies in the rear yard; or the offender killing my partners and then trying to kill me, resulting in a shootout. The nightmares were so detailed, graphic and disturbing that I would wake up very upset, as if it had really happened.

As my time on the Morcombe case continued, so did the amount of time spent visiting prisons and speaking with depraved sexual offenders, most of whom just wanted their five minutes of fame. We also spent a considerable amount of time in the prisons speaking to other violent offenders about information they had in relation to Daniel's disappearance or information they had heard inside from other offenders.

It was times like this that you would stop and realise that your life could change in a heartbeat; one wrong comment or question could result in a prisoner really hurting or killing you. I can recall one such time where I had this feeling, as myself and another detective were speaking to a prisoner. The normal room was not available, so we were taken to a spare room. Myself and my partner were in a fully enclosed room with a violent sexual offender. Sitting back looking at this guy, I could see that he was over six feet tall with a strong build. His hands were massive and when asked, he was very comfortable telling us that he had no issues in prison with people picking on him. As I looked around the room it dawned on me that there were old pieces of equipment lying on the floor. This included metal pipes and pieces of broken furniture. The door was closed and there was no guard watching over us or anyone ready to come to our aid if it all went bad.

That is when the gravity of the situation really hit me. We were in a room with no windows, we had no weapons, no guard watching us, with a violent sexual offender who could literally kill both of us with his bare hands, before we would even make it to the door to call for help. He had been sentenced to twenty-two years of jail time with no parole for committing a series of extremely violent sexual assaults, so he had nothing to lose by assaulting or killing us if we upset him. Trust me, this is when your detective training, people, and emotional intelligence skills kick in and you have that moment in time when you realise you are not in full control of your life and that keeping someone in a good mood is paramount to your survival.

Due to the high public interest, the Daniel Morcombe case continued and we were able to use some interesting investigative techniques and activities, from using listening devices to doing aerial searches in helicopters and utilising the services of an FBI Profiler; the search for Daniel was relentless. Unfortunately, being relentless in this arena was not without its problems. As time went on, the continued dealing with paedophiles, violent offenders and crimes started to take its toll on me. I started noticing changes within myself, such as being grumpy and short with my family over the most minor of issues, not being able to switch off and get a good night's sleep, increased drinking of alcohol to assist in being able to relax, not wanting to socialise, becoming emotional and even going to the toilet eight times before leaving home for work.

At that time in the Queensland Police Service, speaking up about not dealing with issues did not have the same amount of acceptance or support as it does now. As a detective, you were also looked upon as the elite group who dealt with the serious criminals and cases, so saying you were not coping was not the smartest career move. So, I kept it all to myself. I let it bottle up inside me.

After three years on Operation Vista, I was promoted to the rank of sergeant. With just over eight years of service, I found myself as the youngest operational sergeant by both age and length of service on the Sunshine Coast. Being an operational sergeant with the added bonus of being an appointed detective with that length of service was literally unheard of. I was told by senior officers that it was not possible to be an operational sergeant with just over eight years of service and that I would either sink or swim in a very short timeframe. I can recall one very senior commissioned officer telling me that in his thirty years of service, he had only known of one person in the Queensland Police Service that had made it to that level in a shorter time than myself.

The pressure was on! Being so young certainly had its challenges. I found myself managing officers who were a rank lower than me, but who had in excess of twenty years of service. This was more than double my length of service. Luckily, being an appointed detective was also a positive and my investigative skills, knowledge of the law and ability to talk to offenders came in very handy indeed.

As time went by I found my symptoms persisting and actually getting worse. I found that after going to high-risk incidents, such as people armed with knives, my hands would shake uncontrollably. They would shake that much that I could not write in my police notebook. I had been getting emotional whilst watching certain programs on television for some time, but it was when I started becoming upset when reading certain newspaper articles that my wife piped up and said I needed some help. I knew I needed help, I knew I was not coping. I just didn't do anything about it!

> I knew I needed help, I knew I was not coping.

After just under four years, I found myself relieving up at the next level (senior sergeant). This included stints as both the District Crime Coordinator and also as the on-road District Duty Officer, where you were the most senior ranked operational officer in the Sunshine Coast District for that shift out on the road, making the final decision on all operational matters where required.

As my mental health deteriorated, I knew I could not keep going but I was so scared about what people would think if I put my hand up and let everyone know I was not coping. I had seen other officers go out on stress leave and the stigma attached and the rumours were not something I wanted to be remembered for. I was still the youngest operational sergeant by both age and length of service some four years later and with that came the expectation that I would continue up the ladder in my policing career. But I couldn't!

So, I devised a plan to resign from the police service and start another career, hoping that no one would ever know of my mental health problems and that no one would ever think any less of me. My plan was sorted! I also thought that if I removed myself from the source of my problems (policing), that all my symptoms would simply go away and I would move on with life. How wrong I was! Initially, my plan was working as my symptoms subsided and I embarked on my new career outside of policing, but it was short-lived. Within a number of months, my symptoms returned and I was on a downward spiral.

I started seeing a psychologist and a psychiatrist about my ongoing symptoms, hoping this would sort them out quick smart. I refused to really acknowledge I had a formal mental health problem and refused to even entertain the thought of having to take medication to help me through this tough time. It wasn't until I found myself sitting in front of my treating psychiatrist literally crying my eyes out that he promptly told me in a straight, matter-of-fact way that I was depressed. Not only was I suffering from depression, but I was also suffering from Post-Traumatic Stress Disorder (PTSD) and anxiety, and that until I came to terms with that within myself, nothing would help me get better.

The reality had finally sunk in, my life as a person with a mental health condition had begun. I really struggled with this as I looked on it like a change in social status and something that would follow me everywhere for the rest of my life. I had flashes of what I would say or do when I had to fill out a form anywhere and had to answer the dreaded question, 'Do you suffer from any mental health conditions?' My short-sightedness was consuming me. I put myself in a box thinking that my life was over and I would never be the same again.

> My life as a person with a mental health condition had begun.

As the specialist sessions continued, I grew to accept that I wasn't well. I mean, it wasn't that hard to tell with all the symptoms I was experiencing that I wasn't a hundred per cent, yet still, I managed to continue to work. A few months later, my psychiatrist dropped another bombshell straight on me. He told me I should try taking medication and that taking all the sleeping tablets in the world would not fix my sleeping problems as I simply had a chemical imbalance in my brain. This was something I was desperately trying to avoid. Medication? That is something that only mental health patients took, you know the ones in the institutions. Once again, I was putting myself in a box!

Then out came my detective brain, and I started firing off questions to my psychiatrist. What would they do? How long would they take to work? What would the side effects be? How long would I have to take them for? How would they make me feel? He explained that it would be a trial and error process in finding the right medication that worked for me, along with then finding the right dose. With a no-nonsense, calm voice he went on to say that taking the medication would not make me feel on top of the world or completely normal. You see one of my main issues was that I was not sleeping, this meant that I needed a medication with a slight sedative property, not one that made me feel all happy.

To calm my nerves, he also explained that I may go through a few different medications to get the right one, but that was normal, and it was just a matter of waiting for the "wash out" period to pass (How long the medication takes to get out of your system enough to start taking another one). Walking out of his medical suite with the script in my hand, it became even more real that I wasn't well and that this was something that wasn't going to just pass with a few specialist sessions.

The same self-sabotage started all over again, only this time it was far worse. I found myself really worrying about starting to take medication. These questions were running through my head; What would the pharmacist think of me when I handed over a script for these types of tablets? What if it gave me bad side effects, how would it affect my new job? What would people think of me if they found out I was on medication? What if I had a bad reaction to the tablets?

I bit the bullet, got the medication and started the process of slowly building up the dose. Over the next few months I managed to go through about three or four different types of medication. I discovered that I was quite easily affected by medication and I received a number of not-so-nice side effects, like falling asleep all the time and drooling, right to the other end of the spectrum where I was literally having the shakes and being so hyped up I couldn't drive a car.

Is this what my life was going to be like forever? I felt like I was a broken person and someone who had gone from being a high-achieving career police officer to a hopeless nutcase on medication. As we cycled through the different types of medication, I found myself really struggling at work. My health continued in a downwards spiral and I was finding it ever so hard to pretend nothing was wrong.

One day I was driving my car and I had this overwhelming feeling of doom and that my world was closing in on me. I felt extremely anxious and my feelings of worry started to manifest themselves physically. I pulled over my car and sat there on the side of the road and cried. The devastating feeling of ruin and worthlessness was getting worse and worse and I couldn't control it or get my mind to see reason. I managed to drive to a nearby ambulance station and found myself sitting outside in my car just crying and crying.

What was I to do? I was a mess, but if I got out and went into that ambulance station and asked for help, that was a game changer. I knew I couldn't go back to work in that state and I can still to this day remember sitting in my car thinking to myself, *I am hopeless, this is what my life has come to. Sitting outside an ambulance station balling my eyes out.* Deep down, I knew I couldn't go on and that I needed to go into that ambulance station.

As I pushed the glass door open a female ambulance officer greeted me and asked if I was all right. She could obviously see from my physical appearance that I was in a highly distressed state, but at that time she had no idea what from. So, I blurted it out! The words finally came together and I admitted to her and myself that I was an ex-police officer that was suffering PTSD, depression and anxiety and that I couldn't cope. Being taken to the hospital in the back of an ambulance felt so surreal. I talked with the ambulance officer and explained that I had only ever been in the back of an ambulance as a police officer helping to restrain patients. This time I was the patient!

Too ashamed to speak to my wife, I let the ambulance officer ring her and tell her where I was and what was happening. The gravity of my situation was setting in. What would happen from here? What about my work? How would we pay our bills? Would I ever work again? Yet somehow with all of that going on, I felt a slight sense of relief. I felt like I had finally accepted that I really was not well and that maybe now I would receive some help to get better.

After sitting in the waiting room for an eternity, I was examined by a doctor and once again had to tell the same story I had told the ambulance officer. Having calmed down considerably, I was not admitted to hospital and was advised to go back and see my treating psychiatrist and get my medication sorted. The doctor also told me that I would get better and that this was not something that I couldn't overcome. With that, I contacted one of my friends, who was a sergeant at the station I used to work at, and he came and collected me from the hospital.

It was coming into Christmas in 2010 and there I was, too unwell to continue with my new job and my income protection had expired as I was no longer in the police service. Luckily my mental health conditions were approved by WorkCover Queensland as being linked to my time serving as a police officer and I was provided with a mediocre wage from WorkCover. My quest to find the right medication continued as I found myself a prisoner in my own home, too scared and unwell to go outside and face the real world. At first it was quite comforting, I was getting paid and I was in my own little bubble hiding away in our house. I was able to sleep in until lunchtime, get up and have a hot shower and go back to the comfort of my warm doona. I found myself drinking more and more every night. At first this worked a treat, after a few wines or beers I felt semi-normal and could see some sort of perspective around what was happening.

Unfortunately, as time went on, I needed more and more alcohol to get that slight feeling of normality, and with that came the after-effects. The upset stomach, hangovers and wanting to sleep all day, oh and did I mention that the amount of money I was getting paid from WorkCover started getting less and less. This only served to increase my anxiety levels and add another problem to worry about. As the months went on, I continued to hide out in our house. I had a set routine of taking our son to day care, doing the housework then finding some obscure little out of the way coffee shop where I would hide away from the world, drink coffee and read the paper.

Within five months I had lost about fourteen kilograms. I hadn't been that weight since I joined the Police Academy in 1997 as a twenty-two-year-old. None of my clothes fit me and I looked like a shadow of my former self. I had lost my appetite and whatever I ate came out the other end in a very short period of time. I was that unwell, that for a period of time I struggled to even walk out of our house to check the mailbox. There didn't seem to be any light at the end of the tunnel.

With the assistance of my psychologist, I learnt about positive psychology and how it could help me turn things around. Positive psychology focuses on the things you can do, no matter how small, rather than what you can't do. This started with chunking things down to little bite-sized pieces. Setting myself little tasks to achieve each day and then to be grateful that I was able to achieve them. Challenge one was to successfully walk out and check the mailbox daily. I did say small activities and for me, this is where it started.

> I learnt about positive psychology and how it could help me turn things around.

Secondly, I wasn't to look too far ahead. Rather than worry about where I was going to end up or what was going to happen in the coming months or years, I focused on what I was doing that day and that day alone. Then at the end of the day, I would only think about what I had on the next day and how good it would be to get through that day. It also gave me something to look forward to if I was doing something I enjoyed.

Having lived on the Sunshine Coast since 1993, it was hard for me to go out and have a coffee without bumping into someone I knew, and that was the last thing I wanted to happen. To combat this, I made up and rehearsed my own little story to regurgitate verbatim to anyone that I bumped into who might ask me that dreadful question ... "So what are you doing these days?" Being prepared like this allowed me to venture out into the public arena with a solution in my back pocket should I bump into someone I knew. It wasn't perfect and the first few times I trotted it out, I am sure the people receiving it were left thinking that it was a very poor made-up story. As I became more and more confident getting out, I managed to perfect my story to the point that it was believable.

To clarify things, I didn't have a straight made-up lie about what I was doing. I simply had a story that went something like this ... "I am just having some time out at the moment while I work out what I want to do long-term," or "I decided that last job was not for me so I'm just doing some study at the moment and having a bit of a break". (I did actually do some study towards the end of my time off).

I finally found the right medication with the right dose that allowed me to get some sleep, reduce my anxiety and make me feel slightly human. For anyone that has never taken any mental health medication, I can let you know that it is not a wonder pill. You don't suddenly feel amazing. Some medication can take up to six months to work properly, and as for feeling on top of the world, let me just sort that out for you. When you find the right medication that works for you, it basically brings you back up to just below some sort of feeling of normality. Is medication for everyone? Maybe not. But after going through about five different types of medication, I firmly believe that if you choose to take a medication that you will eventually find the right one for you.

As time passed, I started to work out what was going to help me get my life back on track and what was not. I can say that drinking excessive amounts alcohol and hiding away in our house was not going to get me back on track. With the assistance of my specialists, I started getting back into some exercise. I started out just going for a normal walk and eventually moved to high intensity workouts. This was something that I found made a major difference with my well-being, as intense exercise releases endorphins and a number of other feel-good hormones. I also had a good friend who was a serving police officer who would come and take me out for a mountain bike ride, even if I didn't feel like it.

I got to the point where I could talk to people about what I was going through. Along with taking medication, this was one of my biggest fears. But to my surprise, when I built up the courage to talk openly to people about it, I was blown away by the support I received. I was also shocked to hear how many of my friends I thought would not possibly understand, actually opened up to me and told me how they had also suffered from a mental health condition at some point in their life.

As I got out more and more I also realised the benefits of ocean therapy! Ocean therapy for me was finding a nice private spot at the beach and then simply sitting down and staring at the ocean and the incoming waves. I found this to be quite relaxing and calming. It also allowed me to think that bit clearer about what I had to do to get better. At the same time, I was also starting to identify that some things weren't the same. Yes, there were certain activities that I could no longer do. One of the main changes was my distinct loss of confidence. I can recall driving to the rubbish tip one day with my wife in the car. Despite having driven to the tip hundreds of times previously, I found myself asking my wife which way was the quickest way to the tip? I knew every possible way you could go to our local rubbish tip, but I found myself doubting my own ability to make the right decision.

This flowed over to other activities, like doing our finances. Having worked in a bank for six years straight out of school, I was the one in our relationship who had always managed our finances. It was simply something that I did, and I enjoyed it. Yet when I was unwell, I stopped having the confidence to do this task and it was taken over by my wife. Deep down inside, I felt like I had lost the ability to be the person out in front leading our family, the one making the decisions and saying what we had to do to get anywhere.

As time ticked by and my WorkCover payments reduced significantly, I found myself in a position where I felt a bit stronger and I could get back into some type of work. I had no idea what, but I knew I wanted to do something. Nearly eleven months had passed since I had worked, and I knew it was time. With the thought of returning to the working world, I started applying for jobs in earnest. Writing resumes, getting interviews and promotions was something that I had always excelled at as a police officer. I had prided myself on knowing what to put in a resume and how to give the employer the right information to show that I was the best applicant.

As I smashed out the applications one after another I noticed one consistent theme, I was not getting any replies or being shortlisted for any of the roles I was applying for. So, I upped the ante and applied for more jobs, only to get the same result. Overall, I applied for sixty-seven jobs without getting a single interview or notification that I had been shortlisted - nothing. This was certainly not helping my mental health and just added further stress to our already fragile financial position. Thankfully I was able to work out that throwing the same resume at different job applications and expecting a different result was akin to Einstein's explanation of insanity. So, I took the time to change and tailor my resume for the job or type of work that I was applying for. I was also lucky enough to be put in contact with an organisational psychologist through WorkCover who, along with changing my resume, assisted me with finding some host employment.

After eight weeks, I was offered a position within the host employment organisation and the rebuilding of my life had begun. Starting at the bottom again took a bit of adjusting I must admit, but boy did it feel good having a full-time job. I started to feel that we were going to be okay and that I was once again contributing to society. Within a short period of time after starting my new job, I was shortlisted for two regional manager level positions in a government agency. Obviously changing my resume to suit the actual job description was a right move.

I decided to still go for the interviews and as a result, I ended up placing second and third for those roles, which still gave me a sense that I was on the road to recovery.

With a new career in a totally different area, I felt I had finally come full circle and my life was back on track. I was still struggling at times not being a police officer and I think part of me always will, but I can live with that. I am not the same person I used to be, but that is okay! People often ask me if I miss being a detective and do I think I am the same person I used to be. I will always bleed blue deep down, I'd be lying if I said otherwise.

I haven't changed my lifestyle since leaving the police. I haven't rushed out and started taking drugs or committing crimes. I have, however, opened my mind and broadened my exposure to people from different levels in society. Having hit rock bottom myself, I now have a better ability to empathise with people who have been through tough times, people who I previously would not have found myself associating or talking with. Mental health is a great leveller; it does not discriminate between race, religion, or the balance of your bank account. It, unlike most of our modern world, treats everyone it comes across the same!

> Mental health is a great leveller; it does not discriminate

The last seven years have been extremely challenging. I would easily say they have been the most challenging of my life. But I am a big believer that things happen for a reason, you just have to work out what that reason is. It hasn't all been beer and skittles either since starting that full-time job back in November 2011. Thanks mainly to PTSD, I have had several relapses over the last seven years - each from my inability to handle stress like I used to. The difference is that I know that I can get through these tough times. I know there is light at the end of the tunnel and I know that I am not a second-class citizen for having a mental health condition.

I have learnt what my triggers are and how to identify the signs that I am going through a tough time. I also have not stopped learning and trying different things to assist my mental health and the mental health of others. In February 2016 I felt I was in a place where I could talk to anyone about my previous mental health struggles with the HOPE that sharing my story and experiences may help other people going through a tough time. This culminated with teaching myself how to build a website from scratch using the tried and tested "Dr Google" method. After a few months, my website www.healthymindhealthyfuture.com was born and I started writing about my mental health and unemployment journey.

Adding a Facebook account @hmhfuture a bit after that, I continued to engage with people both within my region and around Australia about mental health. I continued to try different health activities like yoga, meditation and floating in salt-loaded water pods to assist in maintaining my mental health, all to hopefully provide that one bit of information that may help someone. As the articles continued to flow, so did the opportunities to start speaking about my journey. I have been fortunate enough to speak to different businesses, non-profit organisations and also do some one-on-one coaching. As strange as it may sound, I have found the one thing I really miss about being a police officer is helping people. But I have now found a way to do that once again.

Running through the trenches of a mental health condition is bloody hard, trust me, I know first-hand. But what I also know first-hand is that it does not have to be the end for you or your loved one. It does not have to define you or limit what you can do. Sure, some things will be different, and you may not be the same person you used to be, but you know what? That is okay!

www.healthymindhealthyfuture.com
www.facebook.com/HMHFuture/

Trudi Bareham

Stepping Through the Lyme Life: My story of surviving Lyme disease

OUR FIRST CONNECTION

It was just one month after Stories of HOPE started that Stuart Rawlins attended an event in February 2017. He was so inspired that night that when I invited him to speak a couple of months later, he invited his neighbour Trudi Bareham. He had only just found out that she had been unwell. Little did he know that when he stopped seeing the once vibrant and energetic Trudi walking her dog around their street, which was usual custom for her, that she was in the fight for her life behind closed doors after being diagnosed with Lyme disease. As Trudi mentions in her story, her illness not only impacted upon her but also on her hubby and two grown-up daughters. After Trudi shared her story a couple of months later, Stuart commented from the audience in the Q & A time, how sad it was that people can literally be neighbours and not even be aware that someone in their own street is struggling. Trudi inspired many that night not just with her story of healing, but also her journey of great bravery and resilience. She recounts it here...

For many years of my life, I seemed to be plagued with various health problems. This included chronic sinus problems and anxiety, which I suffered from as a teenager. I grew up in the UK and in 1982, I had a bad car accident. I was just sixteen at the time and it left me with constant migraines and severe back pain that came and went for several years, until I had reached a point where surgery looked like it could be the only answer.

The surgery itself came with great risks, including paralysis and no guarantee that it would work or that the problem wouldn't return. Taking all this into consideration and with two young children at the time, I decided to find another option. This included months of dedicated physio exercises that brought great relief and all these years later, I have only had intermittent back problems - really no more than anyone else would have. The other damage resulting from the car accident was debilitating headaches and migraines for twenty-seven years, which I suffered from several times a month. Each headache would last for up to five days. It was this constant suffering which led me on a long search for alternative methods to heal from these headaches.

In 2001, I began study into holistic therapies. I was so excited about this new world, opening doors to a new way of healing. I learnt many therapies and techniques along the way and with each, came a deeper knowledge and understanding that our bodies intuitively know how to heal with the right tools and the very real, deep connection between our emotions and physical body. The more I learnt, the more I was able to join the dots concerning my own health journey, which just fuelled my passion to learn and know more about the role the mind-body connection plays in illness and disease.

> Over the years, I've realised it doesn't matter how much you think you know.

Over the years, I've realised it doesn't matter how much you think you know, or how much you learn through training courses. The real education comes through experience, working with other people and more importantly, our own personal lived experience. Whatever I believed about emotions, health and healing, was about to be seriously challenged as my own journey was about to teach me. In February 2005, a job opportunity for my husband popped up in Australia. I was in a personal growth period and had just read the following quote by Benjamin Disraeli - "The secret of success in life is for a person to be ready for opportunity when it comes." We made the decision to jump at the chance, even though we'd never been to Australia before. We sold up and arrived in Buderim in December 2005.

My headaches continued and after years of searching for answers, Bowen Technique (which originated in Australia) crossed my radar. It was the first and only therapy I tried which worked after twenty-seven years of endless, debilitating headaches. I trained as a Bowen therapist and later attended a Mind Body Bowen workshop, which took the technique to a subconscious and felt body experience level. It literally blew my mind and I couldn't stop talking about it!

Our life and journey begin far before our conscious mind is engaged and the experiences I had during this workshop led me to start asking my mum questions about my birth. I discovered I was born blue, not breathing and the doctors struggled to resuscitate me. I was also a forceps birth fifty-two years ago, when birth traumas were treated very differently. But finding out this information, answered so many questions for me. Forceps delivery is common in headache sufferers. I had a twenty-seven-year nasal spray addiction because I was frightened of not being able to breathe and the actual trauma of the birth, my first life experience, was fight/flight. I now understand how fight/flight became my normal and set the stage for illness and disease to develop in later life. The jigsaw pieces of my health and the emotional connection to my physical suffering were quickly falling into place.

In 2009, my beliefs about the body's ability to heal were considerably challenged when I was diagnosed with aggressive

Rheumatoid Arthritis. My initial symptoms began with a bruised and swollen pinkie finger a few weeks after I had received mosquito and sand-fly bites while out up north of the Sunshine Coast. Back then, I never connected the two things. I began my mission to figure out how I could heal myself and spent hours on the internet looking for natural options, dietary approaches, supplements etc. and was fully determined and convinced I would succeed.

It took three-and-a-half years, with many setbacks and periods of time spent on Prednisone, but I did it! All my pathology was back to normal and I was in clinical remission in as many ways as was possible. I was absolutely elated and very keen to share everything I had learned with other sufferers. An article was run in the local newspaper and I was inundated with phone calls from people wanting to know what I'd done. So, in April 2012, "Natural Ways for RA" began its online presence and my local support group formed a month later. I was in the peak of health, with a great deal of knowledge to share. I was passionate about changing diet for health as well as addressing the emotional elements of health and my experience working as a holistic therapist with patients also confirmed these things were very important.

As I learned more, my passion grew for helping others to heal. The next part of my journey taught me it doesn't matter how much knowledge I have, how much passion I have to heal others, their journey is theirs and each one is totally individual and unique to that person. It's a hard lesson to learn when your intentions come from the heart.

My remission was brief. In early 2013, I became symptomatic once more. I had continued researching the best ways of staying healthy and began making sauerkraut, the superfood for gut health. Sauerkraut, it turned out, was the total opposite of superfood for me, I became constipated and my very healthy diet was no longer working. Everything was hurting, my joints were continually swelling and flaring up, I had migrating pain around my body and then I was diagnosed with SIBO (small intestinal bacterial overgrowth) by a naturopath at the end of 2013.

Sadly, I was then put in the too-hard basket by her because I did not respond to her treatment and she told me all my issues were emotional. By February 2014, the pain was throughout my body. I had become completely OCD about food, frightened to eat almost everything because it felt like I was reacting to all food. On the advice of my rheumatologist, I reluctantly started on Methotrexate and Plaquenil (the first line of medical treatment for Rheumatoid Arthritis) and for six months there was a small improvement, before I went progressively downhill and very fast this time. I could barely walk, move or sleep and the anxiety was terrible. I felt so very toxic. When you are trying everything you can to recover and you just seem to be getting worse, it really takes its toll emotionally.

By January 2015, my health had really deteriorated. I had lost around fifteen kilograms and my list of symptoms was growing continually and now included joint pain and severe swelling in most joints, temporomandibular joint pain (TMJ), migrating joint pain and migrating joint flares, including my jaw becoming misaligned, difficulty eating and intercostal pain, which made breathing feel like I was being crushed. On top of that was fatigue, insomnia, anxiety, intense food fears, resulting from how I was reacting to foods, weight loss, night sweats and burning fevers. My blood felt like it was on fire, yet I felt chilled to the bone during the day. I had blurry vision at times, low blood pressure, hormonal imbalances, crawling sensations under my skin and vibrating through the body as well as muscles wasting.

I became even more obsessed about food because it felt like the only thing I could control, but my digestive system was so compromised that I reacted to everything. My life had spiralled out of control so fast, it was terrifying. Throughout all my research, I was fully aware that viruses and bacteria can cause and trigger auto-immune diseases, something I would ask my GP and rheumatologist about at every visit. I completely believed something was driving this illness and it was frustrating when no one listened. One day I mentioned to a friend that it felt like I had things crawling under my skin. She knew someone with Lyme disease who said the same thing and she found me the details of the Chronic Disease Clinic her friend attended.

> I went there in March 2015 and for the first time, a doctor actually listened to me.

I went there in March 2015 and for the first time, a doctor actually listened to me, believed all the symptoms I was suffering from and referred me for intensive testing. I felt heard for the first time. The clinic also had a naturopath and visits there became part of my treatment process. The next six weeks I spent cleansing - raw garlic cleanses, liver flushes, seven-day water fasting and herbal liver detox herbs whilst waiting for test results and I felt the least toxic I had in a long time. By this time though, I was no longer able to drive and functioning on a normal daily basis was becoming increasingly difficult. Emotionally I was struggling and all the beliefs I had about healing were quickly slipping away.

I had never actually considered that I might have Lyme disease and didn't know that much about it. So, when the results came back in May 2015 that I had Lyme, Q Fever, Mycoplasma Pneumoniae, Bartonella and potentially other co-infections, I was shocked. Lyme is known for being transmitted via a tick bite, I cannot recall being bitten by a tick. My original symptom onset began after the mosquito and sand-fly bites at the end of 2008 and I started connecting the dots. It seemed my original diagnosis of aggressive Rheumatoid Arthritis may well have been incorrect, given what I had just discovered. Even now, nine years on, the joint damage is very minimal and not typical of true RA.

The diagnosis, however shocked I was, was actually a relief and my belief was now that I could start getting well again. This could not have been further from reality as I was soon to discover that the disease I had was not acknowledged as a real illness in

Australia. In fact, it was vehemently denied by the majority of the medical profession and government alike. If I had almost any other diagnosis available, medical help and support would have been readily provided. But not with Lyme disease. Can you imagine what it's like to be so incredibly sick, yet have no support from the medical system? There is enormous anger within the Lyme community because of this and understandably so.

Lyme disease is one of the most horrific forms of suffering, it is literally like being in a living death. The sentence is made so much worse by the denial of this illness and the lack of medical help and support. There are a very few doctors willing to help and who are knowledgeable about Lyme, but many of these are targeted by AHPRA (Australian Health Practitioner Regulation Agency) and have had their licences restricted or their right to practice as doctors removed entirely. I was seriously frustrated about the situation, but was too ill to be angry. I knew my focus had to be on my own recovery. Holding onto anger would only be detrimental at this stage.

I started on a half dose of Minocycline, once every three days and built up to a full dose over a period of four weeks. By the time I was at full dose, I was in excruciating 10/10 pain, 24/7, with burning throughout my body, nerve, muscle and joint pain with flares on top, drenching sweats and no end in sight. I was advised to stop the antibiotics. By the time I was diagnosed with Lyme, I was in chronic late stage, which affects all systems of the body. I was so toxic and unable to detox with the genetic expressions I had, and the damage done by the bacteria. So as the antibiotics killed them off, my body couldn't eliminate the dead bacteria or the toxic by-products they create. The inflammatory storm in my body lasted for over nine months, the end of which I was back to the baseline awful way in which I had first arrived at the clinic in March 2015.

I continued to work with the naturopath I met at the clinic and started on anti-microbial herbs (approximately a month after stopping antibiotics) - the usual dose of five milligrams three times a day was still causing massive die-off on top of the inflammatory storm I was still suffering, so I had to micro-dose the herbs. I continued to follow food-based cleansing protocols, ate only cooked foods as my digestive system couldn't break down anything else, had bone broth three times daily for around eighteen months (I can't bear the smell of it now!) and took supplements to support all the genetic issues I had as well as addressing other body systems. All this was done a little at a time and as my body could cope with it.

Despite doing all these things, I continued to deteriorate. It's hard to describe just how hopeless and despairing my life had become. I barely slept. I had to use my face as a lever to get myself out of bed due to the pain and weakness in my body. Every morning I would scream, sob and swear with frustration. Just trying to put my bra on took at least ten minutes, getting dressed was a marathon task filled with pain, and I could barely hold a toothbrush to clean my teeth. The fatigue and pain were relentless, but the mental cost was just as high. I had lost my independence, my ability to function as a normal person. Life as I had known it seemed to be gone. I could so easily have become bedridden, but something within me forced me to get out of bed every day, however hard it was.

By September 2015, my Lyme GP, with all the knowledge and skills he had, told me my best HOPE of recovery was hyperthermia treatment in Germany. I was beyond his scope of knowledge; he referred to me as his patient who had tried everything. Of course, no one has tried everything even if it feels like we have. I was devastated and cried endlessly on top of the normal daily tears. After researching hyperthermia, I could see the success rates weren't what I hoped for. The cost was in excess of $40,000 for two weeks of treatment, plus ongoing costs afterwards and it meant serious consideration.

I was incredibly sick by now and to travel to Germany and undergo such intensive treatment felt as if it would be more detrimental to my health, especially considering the reaction

I had to the antibiotics, which I still hadn't recovered from. I felt like all the beliefs I'd had about my body's ability to heal had been annihilated by this illness. But somehow, somewhere inside me, a little spark of intuition told me hyperthermia was *not* the right treatment for me. After a long chat with my wonderful naturopath, who fully agreed with me, we decided to continue with the protocol I was on, cleaning up my body from the inside and supporting all body systems as required along the way. My trade-off for not going to Germany was a Far Infrared Sauna, which I used daily for the first year and continue to use four to five times a week. I feel it played a significant part in removing toxins, lowering pain and disrupting the bacteria cycle through the increase in body temperature. These bacteria thrive in low oxygen and low body temperature environments.

The most important thing for me at this time was the ongoing support of my naturopath, the belief that the treatments were working and firmly believing that I would get well. Having that at a time when I truly thought I would never recover was priceless. I would have times when the pain dropped to a six or seven out of ten and I believed that was the day I was starting to recover - only for me to crash again within an hour or two. It's amazing to me though, that no matter how many times this happened, the HOPE and belief was always fresh, as if I was experiencing it for the first time all over again.

My lowest point came around October/November 2015. I had absolutely nothing left in me, I couldn't think, worry or focus on anything. I was in the most awful place imaginable. Every day was about survival, yet every day was a living death. This illness was not just affecting me, but everyone close to me was suffering too. I can imagine nothing more brutal than watching someone you love suffer so terribly and be unable to relieve their suffering. My darkest, yet most honest moment, was the day I told my husband I didn't want to be alive in this world anymore. The pain, the suffering, the hopelessness was just endless. All my life I had buried how I felt about things, putting on a brave face so no one worried. Now, there was nothing left to hide behind, this disease had stripped me bare and uncovered things about myself hidden deep within my subconscious.

> I gave my body the permission it needed to start healing.

I had absolutely no other options left other than to surrender to the process and trust it would work. There were no positive feelings, no fight, no trying - just allowing. I believe by surrendering to "what is", and coming to a place of acceptance, I gave my body the permission it needed to start healing. It took a long few months for me to see results, but I am so grateful for the gift of surrender.

At the beginning of January 2016, I began to have small improvements. As well as following an exclusively naturopathic treatment for Lyme, my naturopath was happy for me to start medical Orencia infusions for the Rheumatoid Arthritis aspect in order to give my body a break from the pain and inflammation, potentially encouraging healing. Because of all the detoxing, herbs and supplementary support I had been doing, I feel the Orencia was able to work. Had I tried it when I was very sick, I would have been so immunosuppressed, I shudder to think what might have happened.

Recovery has been slow and steady. I consider the approach I took to treating my body as a whole, as well as addressing the Lyme and co-infections with pulsed treatment, weekly biofilm busting days and daily saunas, a success. Back in July 2017, I had my first major setback with a month-long flu which triggered PTSD around being so ill and I developed severe anxiety. I undertook a series of Kambo treatments (frog medicine from native America), to further help my recovery. The anxiety went after the first treatment in December of that year and the following treatments helped with spiritual growth and recovery, but not the physical symptoms as I had hoped. In April 2018 I had a second setback following a couple of mosquito bites, which triggered a lot of pain and other symptoms, but I have learnt much on this journey. Strength and resilience are within me.

The hardest times in our lives are the times where we grow the most. It doesn't matter how many skills you have acquired, how much knowledge you have, there are experiences in life which render everything you know useless. Lyme disease did that to me. It has been an astonishing teacher for me. No one chooses to suffer so terribly, but I am incredibly grateful for the experience and for what I have learnt. My whole life was taken from me and because of this, I realised just how much in life we take for granted. The beach is my happy place, but I could only watch from afar when I was really sick. I noticed things like how people walked and chatted at the same time without acknowledging how easy this was. People rubbing sunscreen effortlessly over their body, holding a cup in one hand and drinking it easily, when for me, drinking was a major and painful two-handed exercise. I began to see the joy in my simple moments in life, to be grateful for these things. Every day now, I stop and smell the roses - literally, I have a neighbour who grows them!

> The hardest times in our lives are the times where we grow the most.

There are some things I knew before which I still truly believe - our bodies have the ability to heal. The role our emotions play and how the traumatic events can shape our lives. This also includes the smaller daily traumas, which change the homeostatic state of the body and therefore set the precedent for disease. Recovery is far more likely when a fully holistic approach is taken - with any chronic illness.

As the world continually becomes more advanced, complex and stressful, I have discovered that stripping life back, learning basic skills like deep breath work, meditation and just spending time in nature, are the things which can help prevent disease taking hold. Add to this exercise, a nurturing diet, loving relationships and being part of a community of wonderful people and you find that these are the very things that provide the basis for a healthy, happy life. When we love and nourish ourselves first and foremost, our tank is full to share with others. I have no expectations in life nowadays. Having expectations only hindered my recovery and placed limitations on the outcome. Without them *anything* is possible.

www.facebook.com/trudi.bareham

Darron Eastwell

One Life-Changing Moment:
The day I broke my brain

OUR FIRST CONNECTION

The Day I Broke My Brain was the headline I saw when I turned my phone on one morning and saw the local Sunshine Coast Daily web page. Darron had just released his book about a brain injury he sustained after a bike accident and still had a huge journey ahead. Having previously met someone else who had also suffered a traumatic brain injury and had come out the other side, I thought maybe Darron might appreciate meeting another person who understood what he was going through. Someone who could encourage him on the journey ahead. Someone who could give him HOPE. I tracked Darron down on Facebook and reached out to him. Along with being so grateful, Darron instantly expressed his desire to share his miraculous story of survival in person. We instantly clicked and since that day, Darron has travelled the Stories of HOPE journey with me and supported me in helping others find motivation and inspiration. This is how his life changed in an instant, in his own words...

It was May 23, 2015 and I had prepared myself for a day of mountain bike riding at Tewantin National Park, which is located on the Sunshine Coast in Queensland. It was a great day for riding. The sun was shining, with the day's outlook being fine and sunny, as it is most days on the Sunshine Coast. Little did I know that this was the day that would change my life.

My mountain bike speedo indicated that I had been riding for a couple of hours through the national park and I was mainly riding slowly, climbing the steep hills only travelling around eight to ten kilometres per hour. But all of a sudden, the speedo showed a rapid increase in speed as I must have commenced a steep descent. My speedo changed from seven kilometres per hour to about sixty kilometres per hour in a distance of only 500 metres and that is where and when it happened. I had crashed my mountain bike and apparently used my head as the brake to slow down. In that instant, I gained life membership into what's called TBI -Traumatic Brain Injury - and my life would be drastically changed forever.

What I also gained from my new TBI membership was a severe brain injury called Diffuse Axonal Injury, an induced coma for seven days, a fractured skull, a wedge fracture to my T7 vertebra, a fracture to my neck and Post Traumatic Amnesia, which would affect my memory to the point of having zero recollection of that day, including the accident, where it happened, how it happened, the pain I was in, the ambulance ride to ICU and being admitted to three different hospitals over two months. The only fading memory I have been able to retain is in a dream-like form and it happened in the week that I was being discharged from hospital after I had met the doctor's recovery expectations. At that stage, I could leave hospital to continue my rehab and recovery as an outpatient.

To assist in improving my memory, speech and fine motor skills, I was advised by my occupational therapist to write a daily journal of what I had done or was supposed to do during the day. I still can't remember to this day when I started writing my journal. However, very slowly, the words started coming out and I then tried to put them down on paper. My handwriting was just another thing that had been affected by the TBI. Before the accident, I had very neat handwriting and could write very quickly and legibly. But now it was the complete opposite - messy, full of spelling mistakes and not flowing, just like my new speech. Forget trying to use a computer, I was no good at that either. I had forgotten how to use the computer and was no longer familiar with the keyboard.

So, old school, I persisted with my new chicken-scratch handwriting. I tried my best to remember and write down my thoughts. I don't know how long I had been writing my journal for, it could have been about six months, but I could sense some improvement with my writing, language, speech and concentration. My memory and fatigue were still so bad, but I had read several books about TBI survival and recovery to boost my understanding of what was happening. I had never heard or read about TBI prior to my own journey and I said to myself, "Darron, you need to write a book about your own TBI story as it will help you, but more importantly could help other TBI survivors and their families that are going through what you have gone through." This is when *The Day I Broke My Brain* started on paper.

I re-read my journal notes as often as I could (as I couldn't remember what I had written) and then I would jot down chapter suggestions to write about. One day, I just started writing and it took me about twelve months to complete the project, which was something that was completely new to me. Then, since I had handwritten my story, I realised I would need to be able to email what I had written to a publisher. My next step was to type up my scribbly handwritten notes into a more readable format. I began to type daily and set myself a goal to have it completed within a month.

The typing itself was very much a form of rehab and mental stimulation at the same time. As rewarding as it was, after a couple of long days of typing I suffered from bad neuro fatigue, which would knock me out for days and I wasn't able to complete any typing as I was so mentally exhausted. This occurred a few times during the process of typing up the book, so I learnt to take the required breaks to recover and then I would start again, being so determined to finish.

After about one month of typing up my words, I had my first draft. I was feeling proud of myself for completing this task while still navigating the daily challenges the TBI presented me with. It was one of the most satisfying things that I had done in my life. My next thought was, "Who do I contact to try to get it published?" as I did not know the book industry or anyone in the book business. It was then that I thought of David Grant from TBI HOPE & Inspiration in the USA, whose books I had read. I had followed his page on Facebook and received their monthly electronic distribution magazine, which had helped me during my rehab and recovery as well as making me realise I was not alone in living with a TBI.

David is also a TBI survivor and after a few emails were exchanged, we agreed we should work together and get my story into a book format. I still can't believe it really, that I have a book about my own TBI story. And I have had feedback from readers from all over the world about how it has helped not only those on their own TBI journey, but also their families. It provides readers with a window into what a TBI patient experiences so they can understand the complexities of the injury as well as provide them with HOPE, motivation or inspiration to keep positive and push themselves during their own or their loved one's recovery process. Also, they may find help by reading which things I had success with during my rehab and recovery.

I have a picture in my lounge room that I would look at and read on a weekly basis. It says:

> *Sometimes the best thing you can do is not think, not wonder, not imagine, just breathe and have faith that everything will work out for the best.*

I used this statement as a kind of mental note to just live in the moment and not look too far ahead during my recovery and I still do it to this day. I believe that everything in life happens for a reason. I often say to myself I could have survived my TBI to maybe help others. My recovery is still ongoing and I love my life as I am one of the lucky ones.

> I believe that everything in life happens for a reason.

While I was in hospital, I was determined to recover to the best of my ability from my life-changing brain injury and when I was discharged from hospital early on in my recovery, I started using some alternative therapies, which I continue to use today. Some of the different therapies that I have used during my recovery include natural supplements. While everyone has their own views on the best treatment methods to employ in their recovery, I have personally chosen to go down the natural route. My wife strongly felt that by using a naturopath, I may have a better result, so I gave it a go.

This is not the path I am suggesting for everyone and each person needs to be guided by their own health professional, as there is definitely a need in many instances for people to take prescribed medications. So we made the appointment to see a local naturopath and they highly recommended using several different types of natural supplements that have assisted in eliminating my dizziness and improving my speech as well. I know this because when I have run out and have to wait sometimes a few days for more of these supplements, I feel the dizziness and my stuttering speech returning.

Daily exercise also played a huge role in my recovery. I have always enjoyed exercise and it was a large part of my life, so exercising is not work for me. I try to do at least thirty minutes of exercise each day as a minimum. My exercise routine has slowly increased over the last two years as early on, I was so fatigued and dizzy even before exercising, so I was restricted to what I could do. But over time, I would set goals like improving my endurance, fitness, strength and my balance as well as slowly increasing how long the work-outs would go for.

I first started my cardio workouts by using a stationary exercise bike; however over time I improved my balance and cardio so that I could then progress to include a treadmill for walking as well. Fast forward two-and-a-half years in my TBI recovery and I am able to use an exercise bike, rower, incline stepper, treadmill and free weights in cardio and strength workouts at my gym, which I try to do at least three times per week. I also like to do some swimming.

I was advised by a healthcare professional that listening to music or playing a musical instrument is good for brain recovery after a TBI and is one of the only things that lights up the entire brain. I have always loved music and after hearing this, I decided to learn the guitar and now take music lessons. I have incorporated listening to music and learning the guitar into my recovery process as well. Music is good for the soul; they say it can be so uplifting, and it puts you in a great mood and can help energise you as well.

> I have tried to incorporate as much laughter in my day as possible.

I have tried to incorporate as much laughter in my day as possible. Again, it's an uplifting activity that doesn't cost anything and helps with your mood. So I try to laugh as much as possible.

My wife had previously known about the benefits of using essential oils and when I was in my coma; she had researched which essential oils could benefit my injured brain. I was lucky to have had my wife, who had found out that frankincense was good for treating any kind of brain injury as it was the only essential oil that can penetrate the brain barrier. She made sure I received daily frankincense, even while in a coma. I also use peppermint and lavender to assist with my daily headaches or concussion-like symptoms.

I was never a big reader before my accident, having only read the books I was required to read in high school. However, I was willing to do anything to help with my recovery and my memory, so I constantly read books, used Facebook to keep up with things, searched information about TBI or things that I was interested in on the internet and read about as much as I could. It helped me so much with my verbal skills, communication, spelling, re-learning my computer skills and retaining information. My memory improved as well.

I would attempt to do meditation during the day to just relax and calm my mind and body and remove the negative energy or thoughts that I was having. For a long time, I didn't know what happened to me or if I was going to be okay. To assist with sleep, I complete a technique called Yoga Nidra which is a form of guided relaxation meditation. All these therapies have helped with my own recovery and I continue to see small improvements with my cognitive functions, memory, fitness and my guitar playing, which just shows that it is helping me in the healing process one day at a time.

www.darroneastwell.com.au
www.facebook.com/darroneastwellsTBIJourney/

Shelley Ross May

Learning to Love Yourself: The truth about my battle with bulimia

OUR FIRST CONNECTION

It was the first time I had attended a business network meeting at the Headland Golf club back in 2015. It was a very early start time for me – 7 o'clock in the morning to be exact - and not the time of day when I am at my best. In fact, I was still half asleep. But as I walked in, I saw this beautiful lady dressed up in colourful clothes and she seemed to be very bubbly and awake. I asked her where I could get a coffee immediately! We instantly gravitated towards each other because I am a colour fanatic as well. We were also both in the early days of trying to get our businesses off the ground and we found that we had quite a bit in common. As a result, we have been close friends ever since. It was some time, however, before Shelley revealed to me her secret - that she was living with bulimia and had done so most of her life. Some months later, after she started to experience a breakthrough, I invited her to share her story to inspire others who may be going through a similar journey. Here is her very transparent and powerful story...

My battle with bulimia started when I was about seventeen. At first, I would make myself throw up when I'd had dessert or if I felt I'd eaten too much. For as long as I can remember, I have had body image issues, always feeling fat and much bigger than all my friends. I became obsessed about being thin, constantly watching what I ate, counting calories and forever on some "fad" diet or another to try and lose weight. I'm not sure how I first found out about bingeing and purging, but it felt like a win-win at the time, because I could eat whatever I liked but then get rid of it. For the first few years I didn't do it every day, but fairly regularly when no one was watching, or when I was on my own.

It got progressively worse when I went overseas to the UK. I decided to open up and tell my flatmate because I thought if she knew about it, it would make me less likely to do it. That worked for a while, but then I would always find a way to purge, even if it meant making an excuse to go out so that I could go to public toilets. I decided to go and see my GP, who referred me to a psychiatrist. This would be the first of many I would see over the years. What I found from this source was that, whilst they gave me possible reasons for why I was doing it (I was sexually abused as a toddler by my step-father and often told I was fat, which would have created self-worth and body image issues), they didn't give me the strategies or support to move past it. I almost felt justified in doing it, because I felt sorry for myself for the way I had been treated. And so, it continued.

> The worst things about a mental illness like this is that it feels like you have no control.

One of the worst things about a mental illness like this is that it feels like you have no control over your mind. I would wake up in the morning and be absolutely determined not to do it on that day. I was taking a contraceptive pill in the morning, so I knew that I couldn't purge before it was absorbed into my body. Around about 11 a.m., this little voice in my mind would say, "Okay, it's safe to do it now Shelley – go on – just one more time," and on and on it went. I would always give into it and off I would go compulsively to the grocery store and takeaway shops. I would buy foods that I knew would come up easily, and then I would go home and eat them all in a very calculated way before throwing them up. I was spending £20 to £30 a day on food that I was throwing up. Wasting money that I really didn't have would make me feel so bad and so guilty, so much so that I would then punish myself for being so weak by doing it all over again the next day.

It was such a vicious, never-ending cycle. I hated myself for doing it. I would often be bent over the toilet, sobbing and feeling so hopeless and desperate. It came to a point where I couldn't gag anymore. The corners of my mouth were often cracked, my eyes were always bloodshot from the pressure, I had huge lumps on either side of my throat and I had a nasty callous on my hand where my teeth dug into it when I was purging. Very raw details, but very much the sad reality of how I was living on a daily basis. I reached out to a couple of friends hoping for support, but they were very judgmental and disgusted by my behaviour. I felt very alone.

I got a great job as an air hostess and started travelling abroad, but the situation became progressively worse after that. There was such a huge emphasis on what you looked like and what size you were, so it made me even more self-conscious about my body. The fact that I felt my body didn't match up to anyone's expectations, especially mine, and because I lived on my own and had no one to answer to, I started purging up to five or six times a day.

I married at the age of thirty-seven and the eating disorder carried on in varying degrees. Sometimes there would be weeks when I wouldn't do it at all and then I would do it every day for a month. I am a comfort eater, so it was always worse when I was in stressful or emotional situations. There were times when I could control it and not purge at all; for example through both of my pregnancies where I felt I had an excuse to let my weight go unchecked. Then once my child was born, I would be desperate to lose all the baby weight and the cycle would begin all over again.

> I felt like a failure. Shame was my constant companion.

It carried on right throughout the years my two children were growing up. I hated and resented being in the kitchen and having to cook for my family. Food was basically my enemy. I cooked the easiest meals, usually out of a box or packet because I wanted to be in and out of the kitchen as quickly as I could. Because I always had chocolate, lollies, biscuits, crisps, etc. in the house for me, my children grew up eating a lot of sugar and processed foods. As a parent I felt like a failure. Shame was my constant companion.

I started becoming increasingly aware of the terrible example I was setting for my two children, particularly when my daughter started going through puberty. I watched how hard it was for her to cope with the same body issues I had struggled with and realised that I had done nothing to help her. In fact, I had probably made it worse for her. Food and weight consumed my thoughts and, looking back now, I am heartbroken at the amount of time I wasted thinking about myself and not about my children.

When I was fifty-one, I started a health and wellness business from home and the company I was working with released a weight management programme. To enable me to market it effectively and ethically, I wanted to try it myself, know that it worked and understand the "whys and wherefores" of it. It was a three-month program, which I followed to the T. I believe that participating in and following this program was what broke the cycle/habit of bingeing and purging for me. Since coming off the program I have been determined to change and I am concentrating on cooking healthy food from scratch. I am actually enjoying spending time in the kitchen now. My daughter and I often cook together and it has become a creative experience that makes me feel a whole lot better about myself, especially in my role as a parent. We sit down and eat meals together as a family now, which we never used to do, and I love that so much.

I have spoken openly to my family, and especially my children, about the eating disorder and have apologised to them for the example I have set them regarding food. They have been incredibly understanding and empathetic and I am hoping that by speaking to them honestly and openly and explaining my journey, they will be deterred from ever going down the same path as I did. Although I haven't purged for about two years now, the eating disorder mentality still stays with me. I think it's a bit like what people say about alcoholics – they are only ever one drink away from starting again. That's how it feels for me.

There are often times, when I feel I have overeaten, that I am tempted to purge. But now I have the strength to keep that in check, which is extraordinarily liberating. My faith has played a huge part in my continuing recovery and I spend time every day listening to inspired personal development podcasts. I do believe I am a lot further along in my journey of learning to accept myself as I am and in learning to love myself which, I think, is key to overcoming any eating disorder.

The reason why I haven't spoken out about it, and shared my story before, is because I didn't have a specific plan of how to stop bulimia, so I didn't feel qualified to help people in any way. However, I do believe that when I was going through it, having had someone to talk to who had bulimia, or who'd had it and been able to overcome it, would have made all the difference in the world to me. Just to have had someone to talk to who I felt didn't pass judgment on what I was doing and who completely understood what I was going through. For this very reason, I want to be that person for others.

I really believe that God allows us to go through painful things in order for us to help others who may be going through similar trials. I love this saying: *People don't always need advice. Sometimes all they really need is a hand to hold, an ear to listen, and a heart to understand them.*

I also want to be available to help parents and to give them some understanding of what it is like to live with bulimia. After all I have been through, I am able to make them aware of some of the signs and symptoms to look out for if they suspect their child is struggling with an eating disorder. It just could be the very thing that helps save a life from the same world of pain that I have lived through.

I run an anti-aging, health and wellness business from home, which has been incredibly instrumental in my healing process. The results I have had personally, not only with the weight management program, but also the skincare and health supplements, have changed my world, my perspective on life and, most importantly, of myself. I have so much more confidence and self-belief, which has really helped me want to change and become a better version of myself in all areas.

I am so excited about my future. As I am able to run the business on my terms, I can spend time with my children after school, help them with their homework and take them to afternoon activities. I can schedule time with my husband, who works away from home, and now have the financial potential to provide more freedom and choices for my family and to bring my husband home, so that we can all be together. At the same time, I am fulfilling my deep desire helping others to achieve their hopes and dreams. This is something that gives me an incredible and very real sense of purpose. It also enables me to allocate time to people who may need my help or support with eating disorders. I would also love to become a part of an Eating Disorder Support

Group for older sufferers, perhaps giving them the HOPE they are often so desperately looking for.

One thing I would like to leave with you is this... Don't let the *reason* you do something be the *excuse* that keeps you doing it.

www.nsinsider.com/intro/
www.facebook.com/evenyoungerthanyesterday

Denise Dielwart

Healing grief, one widow at a time

OUR FIRST CONNECTION

Things really seem to have a domino effect. Especially in this case. I had met Denise one day at Shelley's house. I thought Denise was lovely, but she had a sadness about her. As we took our seats together, sinking into the large leather lounge to watch Shelley do a Nu Skin demonstration and show us the latest and greatest products she was selling, Denise opened up and shared her heartache with me about how she had lost her husband suddenly at the age of fifty-two. Some months later, and after she found great healing from grief, I invited Denise to share her very moving story of how she came out the other side of the grieving process and how she has found passion and purpose through her pain. These days she is working with widows all around the world helping them heal. In this chapter, the founder of Living Beyond Grief and Loss shares her emotional, yet healing, process...

It is only when we share our story that we can create healing and change. So here is the story of how I suddenly became a widow at the age of fifty-two. It begins when Maarten and I met. I was sixteen, I was still at school, and he was nineteen, fresh out of the army in South Africa. Conscription was in place in the '70s and every male over the age of sixteen had to do army duty and they were often sent to the borders of Angola and Namibia to protect South Africa.

We met at my best friend Joey's sixteenth birthday party and it was love at first sight for him, but not for me. I thought he was weird! It was the days of flower power. He had long, untidy hair, funny purple flares that were way too short and a bright green shirt. I won't even mention his shoes (they came from the Angolan border where he had just completed his army training). He was *not* my type at all. I was too cool for that. Maarten persisted and persisted and persisted in pursuing me. When he came over, I even hid in cupboards pretending I was not home, but he was not a quitter and was not going to take no for an answer. Needless to say, I fell in love with this crazy Dutchman.

In 1976 we got married and in 1977 we moved to Holland to live. Maarten had always heard stories from his parents about how fantastic Holland was, so at the age of nineteen and twenty-one we packed up and left South Africa for our Dutch adventure and our new life began. There I fell pregnant with my first daughter. I really missed my mum and friends in South Africa, so after only twelve months we returned to Johannesburg. It was a fun time back then in South Africa, where we built our first home. My mum moved in with us and we had two more children, my son and our second daughter.

In the early '80s, trouble, unrest and terrible events began in South Africa. Rioting and burning began in the townships and it was no longer a safe place to live or call home. Our business backed onto the Alexandra Township, which was a dangerous place with burnings happening daily. It was the time of Winnie Mandela's terrifying Necklace Murders. The army used our business as a stop, therefore we had a lot of inside information about what was really happening. We even had a petrol bomb thrown into our business. We knew, for the safety of our children, we had to leave South Africa and start over. Finally, on November 27, 1988, after a two-year wait for immigration approval from Australia, we packed up everything and we started our new life in Perth, Western Australia, with just $4500 to our name, no jobs and not knowing anyone. Armed with just a massive dream and HOPE for our future, we looked forward to greater days ahead.

As with all relationships, we experienced ups and downs over the years, but we somehow managed instead of growing apart to grow stronger together. We worked and were together side-by-side twenty-four hours a day in everything we did, which included our many businesses and our down-times of fun and play. We did nothing without each other. We were each other's world. Maarten was my rock and I was his. Maarten always told me that I was the love of his life. I was so blessed to have him in my life and he was an amazing father. Within the first year of immigrating to Perth, my mum passed away unexpectedly of cancer. She was only fifty-seven and it hit me really hard. It was only six weeks from the time she was diagnosed until she passed away. It happened so quickly that I had little time to even process.

I was absolutely shattered, and being an only child, I had no siblings to share my grief with. My dad had passed away fifteen years earlier and for the first time in my life I felt like an orphan, even though I was married with three children. I was very alone in the grief I suffered as a result of losing my mum. Even though I had Maarten, who was my rock and supported me and my children through this time, I still felt so alone.

Over the years of working together, we started three businesses and sold three businesses, which saw us move around Australia - from Perth in Western Australia to Coolum Beach on the Sunshine Coast in Queensland. I always dreamed of living on the Sunshine Coast and Maarten dreamed of having land around him. So after five years of living on the Sunshine Coast, we moved up north to a small town called Rockhampton, which is on the Tropic of Capricorn. Here we had the best of both worlds. I loved my time living on the Sunshine Coast so much and as we drove off towards our new destination up north, past beautiful Coolum Beach, I looked at the ocean with tears running down my cheeks and I said, "I will be back – I don't know when, I don't know how, but I will be back." What I didn't know at the time of making my promise, was that I would return as a widow ten years later.

In 2005 we designed and built our forever dream home just north of Rockhampton on eight beautiful acres surrounded by natural bushland and many, many gum trees, birds, parrots, and kangaroos. There was a huge pool and a motorbike track complete with jumps. It was our fun home built and designed with love for our three kids and eight grandsons to enjoy with us. Life was perfect. By this time, the kids were independent with their own families and had their own homes and now it was finally Maarten's and my time together. Time to really start living our lives without the stress of supporting a family. We were both young, I was forty-eight and Maarten had just turned fifty-one; we had a whole new life ahead of us, finally. Never did I ever imagine that just four years later, at the age of fifty-two, I would be on my own trying to make sense of what just happened.

In May 2009, my life changed forever. Maarten passed away suddenly and without warning – it was not supposed to happen. He was only fifty-five and healthy. Never sick a day in his life. I was the one with Rheumatoid Arthritis, aches and pains, but he was strong, healthy and loved life. He was my rock. I went into complete shock and disbelief. It was like I was living in a complete fog and had totally lost my sense of self and my self-worth. I had lost half of me that day. The love of my life. The one person that loved me unconditionally

> It was like I was living in a complete fog.

and everything about me, the good stuff and the not so good. I don't remember much of the months that followed after Maarten passed away. If you were to ask me what day his funeral was on, I couldn't tell you. You would have to ask my daughter. It's just a blur.

It was a normal Monday morning, and we both had appointments to see clients. Maarten was about to leave as I was getting ready. We said our usual 'goodbyes, have a great day and see you later' About half an hour after Maarten had left, I got a phone call. It was him calling to say he was coming home and could I please phone the doctor as he had a terrible backache. He never made it home. Instead, he collapsed on the side of the road and was taken by ambulance to the Rockhampton Base Hospital, where he was immediately flown by Royal Flying Doctors to Brisbane. My daughter and I arranged commercial flights from Rockhampton and arrived in Brisbane in the early hours of the morning. Maarten had already had surgery on his back and was in ICU. I was numb from shock and disbelief, simply going through the motions of what's next, what's next, one foot in front of the other. At this point, I had no idea why or what had happened.

The doctors and specialists soon came into ICU and explained that Maarten had had a spontaneous bleed of his spine; a one in a million occurrence. This only happens if an epidural or lumbar puncture goes wrong, and he'd had neither. It was a complete mystery. He was paralysed from the waist down because of the pressure of the bleed on his spinal cord. I was in complete shock at what I was hearing, but he was alive, and if he never walked again, I would love him through it. After the first day in ICU, he moved his big toe and my daughter and I were comforted with the thought that he was going to be okay. After all, he was a fighter and had always had such a positive outlook on life.

Maarten was then transferred to a general ward and started physio. He had to learn to walk again. He jokingly said that he was not pole dancing, but pole walking. His sense of humour and positivity were so inspirational for me. He was getting better day by day and making great progress. I was so happy, he was coming home! I was unable to stay with him in Brisbane as I had to keep our business running, so I travelled the eight-hour journey to Brisbane each week, sometimes twice a week, staying with him at the hospital on the weekend.

Two weeks after he collapsed and was admitted to the Brisbane hospital, and after our usual 7.30 p.m. phone call, he said he was a bit tired and we would chat in the morning. At 11 p.m. that night, I was woken up by my phone ringing next to me. Groggily I answered to hear a strange voice on the phone asking if I was Denise Dielwart and to hang on for the doctor. The doctor came to the phone and informed me that Maarten had had complications. I asked if he was okay and her reply was, "No – he has passed away from a suspected heart attack."

I screamed and screamed and fell to the floor; this was not happening, how could it? I was just talking to him hours earlier, he had just had a heart cardiology test that day and everything was fine. His blood pressure, his heart, it was all okay. He was meant to be coming home. I don't know how I got the strength to do it, but I then had to call my children and tell them that their dad had just passed away. In that one moment in time, my life changed forever – I became a widow. How was I ever going to carry on with my life without him? I spiralled into a deep pit of grief and depression and my life lost all HOPE and meaning. I started isolating myself, masking my feelings and pretending that I was okay. I was seeing a psychologist who was great, but I was not healing, and counselling was not helping me.

> I spiralled into a deep pit of grief and depression.

To everyone around me, I appeared to be coping so well. But I knew the truth. I was crumbling inside and I felt like I was slowly dying. I missed Maarten so much. My heart ached for him. The dark nights and weekends were the worst; I was so alone in that big house. I was living a lie. I even got involved with someone after eighteen months to somehow show myself, and everyone around me, how great I was travelling and that I was moving on. Needless to say, this relationship did not last long. It was based on a lie - a lie to myself.

I was hurting so much and knew I had to heal inside and I realised that it was up to me to start creating my new future and my new life. I had to start my new book, with my new chapters. The book Maarten and I wrote together was now closed, it closed the day I became a widow. I then refused to become a victim of my grief. My biggest fear was growing old, lonely and bitter and I decided I couldn't let that happen. I started searching for answers. I Googled, I asked people, I joined groups and I read books. Lots of books. I searched and searched for answers and in 2011, I made a life-changing decision.

I embarked on my studies to become a life coach so I could help myself better understand who I was and how to heal myself from the inside out. I knew I had to re-invent me; I had to re-discover my sense of self. I had never lived on my own, as Maarten and I met when I was sixteen, still a child. I had no idea at the age of fifty-two who Denise was. I was no longer Maarten's wife, the kids were all independent, and yes, I was still their mother, but now from a distance. It was just me… but who was *me*?

And so my journey began; I jumped down the rabbit hole. It was all about me. It had to be. I had to heal myself. I had to start living and feeling again. Over the next three years, I learnt about so many things. Human behaviour, emotions, conditioning, beliefs, strategies, the stories we tell ourselves and how they shape our lives, self-talk, thoughts etc, etc. I studied Neuro-Linguistic Programming, hypnosis and EFT (Emotional Freedom Technique). There wasn't much I didn't study. I became so hungry for change and growth. I was diving deep into what made me tick and why I masked my feelings and pretended all was okay.

This was one the hardest and most challenging journeys I have ever undertaken in my entire life. Some days, I was in such a dark place that I would lock myself in my walk-in robe in the dark and cry all day, unbeknown to the outside world. I had so many emotions that I had buried for years that started bubbling to the surface. I experienced emotions that I wasn't even aware of. No sooner would I clear one emotion then *boom*, another one would surface. I was a mess. I cried, I got angry, I felt immense pain and isolation as well as happiness and peace, and I knew that I was healing. I was healing myself, one emotion at a time. This was the beginning of my future and my healing journey. I had committed to myself to heal and live in joy again.

> No sooner would I clear one emotion then boom, another one.

I continued to live in our home, despite struggling mentally and financially to keep the eight acres going, but I loved where I was living and I clung onto the memories with everything I had. I was not left with millions as many people believed I was. I lost half of my income when Maarten passed away and I had to create my own income. I started my business mentoring practice, Bizsolutionz, because after all, I knew business. When I combined this with my coaching skills, I was confident I could help businesses make more money. I did this for six years, but felt empty and unfulfilled.

I was frustrated and started questioning why I was doing this and once more went deep within myself. I did some serious soul searching and eventually had to acknowledge that my passion was not in business, but in helping other widows heal themselves quickly and find their joy journey, just as I had done. This was something I had always wanted to do after Maarten passed away, but like all things, I pushed it away and dismissed it as a pipedream.

During my search for answers, I realised what little help there was for widows. I discovered how misunderstood widowhood is and how often it is compared to divorce and separation. I was asked questions like, "How long did it take you to get over Maarten?" Or people would say things like, "I know exactly how you feel, because my mother died." It still floors me all these years later when I am confronted with these questions or blanket statements. I just smile now because I realise people don't understand unless they have walked in my shoes. Unless the immense deep pain and loss of losing a life partner, the other half of yourself, is experienced, it is absolutely impossible to understand or feel these emotions.

In August 2015, without even batting an eye or giving it much thought, I packed up the house within a month, contacted a real estate agent, found tenants, and moved back to the Sunshine Coast. Without knowing at the time, I had fulfilled my promise to myself exactly ten years after I'd made it. I had forgotten about the promise until a friend and I drove past the exact spot in Coolum Beach where I had uttered those words all those years ago and it all came flooding back to me. I broke down and cried as I recalled that moment. Now I was back, as a widow, without the love of my life. I knew then though, that my life purpose had just begun.

I did the easy thing - I started a free support group on Facebook called Widows Living Beyond Grief and Loss, offering free help and support. I thought a few widows would join, however, within a few weeks it grew to over 1,000 members with widows joining from all over the world. It now has over 3,600 active members and is growing daily. I quickly saw the massive need for deeper, ongoing support for widows, regardless of where they are in the world. I started deep-diving and reflecting on how I healed myself so quickly and what steps I had taken, and realised that it was only when I gave myself permission to feel my emotions, to really feel them on a deep level, and go down into that deep pit of grief, that I was able to let go of my emotions. Only then was I able to overcome the pain and become whole again.

And so my F.L.O.W Method, (Feel, Let go, Overcome, Whole) was born, which is now the foundation of my eight-week online transformational program, Living Beyond Grief. This is truly transformational from the inside out. What makes Living Beyond Grief transformational? After each week, we hop on a coaching call and go down the rabbit hole together to face and heal any emotions that have bubbled to the surface. I would have loved to have had someone hold my hand during that time in my life amid my massive meltdowns and guide me safely through to the other end. Inner transformation only happens with support and love.

I have added five-day Widows Healing Retreats, which take place three times a year. The last retreat was in Phuket, Thailand. What an amazing experience it was for the ladies who chose to join me, all at different stages in their grief journey. There are so many 'aha' moments, tears and deep healing at their core. They all stepped into their Joy Journey, ready to live life on their terms.

My life was forever changed on May 4, 2009. However, the blessing in that was the endless opportunities to be able to support and help widows heal themselves. Here's the thing: if I had not become a widow, I would not be doing what I love now.

www.livingbeyondgriefandloss.com
www.facebook.com/livingbeyondgriefandloss/

Luke Bourne

Bourne For a Greater Purpose: The battle against one of the world's rarest cancers.

OUR FIRST CONNECTION

It was a simple message. I sent my thoughts and best wishes to this stranger, a young guy in the fight for his life, after a post he put up on Facebook. My mum had battled cancer, so I had a sense of the journey he was navigating. Despite what he was going through, I found his attitude of gratitude towards life was so inspiring that a couple of weeks later, I met him up with him and his beautiful wife Rachel in a local cafe. He talked profoundly about something that day which moved me to tears; the fact that through his immense suffering, he had finally learnt the art of self-love, which in turn had led him to see others in a totally different light and taught him the meaning of true compassion. That was my introduction to Luke "the unicorn" Bourne. He calls himself a "proud bogan hippy" because his love for cars and motorsports is equal only to his passion for sharing love in this world of ours. It wasn't long before Luke was sharing his journey at one of my events. It is so inspiring, it had to be included in this book ...

It's December 2014, all is well in Luke's world, he thinks he's happy, having recently come back from a Japanese holiday with his wife Rachel. Little did he know the journey that he was about to embark on with the most beautiful person in the world would change in an instant.

Rachel and I decided to move back to the Sunshine Coast due to environmental/relationship issues we were having in Mackay. The work we were doing and the lifestyle we were leading was taking us down a path that we couldn't continue. We didn't know it yet, but we were looking for happiness and agreed that it was the best option for us as a couple.

I was hell-bent on my career in the mines (which was silly) whilst trying to start and support a family of our own. After three miscarriages, both Rach and I needed support from family, so we took the plunge to move down south closer to that support. Nearly a month after we moved down, I started getting symptoms... I had never even known what a headache was, but after a harsh couple of night shifts putting up with migraines, it had got to the stage where I was unable to fly back to work. After reluctantly taking some sick days off, I made an appointment at the doctor to get to the bottom of what was going on and try and find a solution.

A CT scan showed a large tumour in my brain. Luckily enough, my GP had a mentor who was a neurological brain surgeon and I was able to be booked in for surgery the next week at the Wesley Hospital in Brisbane. After not having much to do with hospitals over my time, I ended up celebrating my twenty-eighth birthday the week before my brain surgery. The doctor was very optimistic and said that it looked like an isolated tumour. The promising news meant there was no extra worry associated with the brain surgery going ahead.

After operating, they discovered that the tumour itself was around the size of a tennis ball and it had actually pushed my brain all the way over to the other side of my skull. This was, literally, the pressure I could feel as well as being the cause of my blinding headaches. The doctor commented on how well my brain had handled the pressure, but also soberly added that I wouldn't have had much time if it hadn't been addressed.

I spent ten days in recovery and then received a bombshell - a diagnosis of Alveolar Soft Part Sarcoma (world's rarest cancer) stage four, and a PET scan afterwards showed the true depth of the physical struggle I was in. There were also two tumours in my right lung, another in my abdominal wall and adrenal gland and a massive one encompassing my pancreas, which was ten centimetres. The primary tumour had been in my right hand, but was misdiagnosed as a rugby injury when I was thirteen years old in Southland, New Zealand.

They were some very tough times in the Wesley hospital. The rarity and type of cancer meant that chemotherapy wasn't an option, and the stage of the disease meant that there was nothing available in the Western medical world. Yup, it was all a bit of a large pill to swallow as we had never had to deal with cancer in our family before. My journey quickly escalated from an isolated issue to becoming the worst stage of cancer possible with no treatment options and an extremely little amount of information to go on.

The hospital was kind enough to allow Rach to sleep with me some nights, as the truth of the situation was unbearable for me at times. I also had my family just down the road, and some relatives travelling from New Zealand to support me.

Even though the brain surgery recovery time had been ten days, I also then had targeted radiation to my brain for two more small tumours that they had found after the wound had healed. Straight after this, I had my primary tumour removed from my right hand. Let's just say it was a decent month-and-a-half just getting that part sorted.

My sister Alisha held a family meeting at her house in Murrumba Downs. My family had been busy researching different protocols from around the world on my behalf and the meeting was to discuss what they had found that had healed other people suffering from different forms of cancer. The love and heartbreak that was expressed around the table that day could not possibly be put into words. I am the youngest of my family with eight, ten, and twelve years the gap between me and Reon, Grey and Alisha respectively.

We had been looking at treatment options at clinics in Europe when we received good news at a follow-up appointment at the Wesley Hospital. My tumours had grown by 10%, but the good news was that phase two of a trial was opening up, which was being held at the Princess Alexandra Hospital in Brisbane. So I left the Wesley and entered the public hospital world and began on the CASPS (Cediranib Alveolar Soft Part Sarcoma) trial in July 2015. The trial was extremely rare and was for the cancer that I had, which was awesome. The doctor said we would be extremely lucky to see another trial open up in my lifetime.

At this stage I was 132kg, I knew nothing about cancer and generally, I was fighting my own brain as the doctors were hesitant about giving me a life expectancy. There was just so little information on the cancer itself. I say *we* changed everything, but it was mostly Rach, my beautiful wife, who took control of looking after me. The drug trial itself was quite harsh on the body, causing constant diarrhea and rapidly reducing my weight as I was dropping a steady one to two kilograms a week.

It was such a difficult time for me and it's so hard to even try to explain the gravity of my thoughts and feelings at the time. But essentially it was me learning or trying to come to terms with the thoughts: "You are going to die, there is no cure for your disease, just a trial that was going to try and inhibit the growth." All at thirty years of age. Then something unusual happened. My mum had made the very casual recommendation that I should go and see my dad's holistic doctor, Dr Sandeep Gupta. This was a "can't hurt" approach, as he had previously had great success in treating my

> You are going to die, there is no cure for your disease.

dad and had taken his Type Two diabetes pills from twenty to zero in just four weeks.

I didn't understand it at the time, but the options that he opened up to me would not only eventually save my life, but also allow me to cope and thrive in a gruelling environment you wouldn't want to wish upon anybody. The next eighteen months of growing and learning whilst trying to make the most of my time was extremely different. I didn't ever get an official timeframe or life expectancy from the doctors, but I was told I was terminal, which is anywhere up to twenty-four months. I do, however, have a letter from two years ago saying that I had less than twelve months to live… It's something I take great pride in proving wrong, along with the regular follow-up survival phone calls from the trial.

Whilst I don't wish to take sides on the Western versus alternative medicine debate, I do share the thought that both sides have helped me stay alive. I had a test done (RGCC) which looked at my sensitivities to natural and Western therapies, how the cancer was travelling and different ways to best make it slow down. It was a very tough/controversial topic to discuss, but at the end of the day, people will have their opinion and I have mine from my own experiences.

You see, the biggest struggle that I have found through all of this is actually living with this illness present in my body. Not only do you have to learn how to best utilise your time while juggling bucket lists, time with loved ones and continuing to try to find a cure, but you must learn how to deal with fear. That fear isn't just your own. It comes from doctors, family members and just about anyone you come into contact with. One of the best lessons taught by my guru Dr G was overcoming the fear of death and learning that I can love more if the result of my death was to happen.

The Cediranib trial lasted for eighteen months and pretty much depleted my body. Overall, it kept my tumours at bay and no new ones had grown, so we were happy with that. I went from being 146kg at my heaviest to just 75kg by the time I had finished the trial. I think officially I started the trial at 132kg, which was still a significant drop in weight. I had constant diarrhea for that time, along with plenty of other side effects like peeling skin and lack of appetite. These to me were just minor effects as I was just happy to be alive. The thing with trials and the hard concept to swallow is that trials only want pure information; you're not actually allowed to do any alternate healing while on it. It's very hard to be restricted when all you want to do is anything to feel better, recover and be happy.

At some stage I believed that there had to be some form of balance attained as a result of having so many major changes to my body. Unfortunately instead of balance, my body went a bit haywire and I suffered a setback of sorts. This happened while we were in Fiji for my best friend's thirtieth birthday. It was my first Tonic Clonic Seizure (one of the worst types, formerly called "grand mal" seizures). It was a traumatic experience that saw me urgently back in the Brisbane hospital the same day. I would go on to have more seizures and it became part of my life. Managing to get enough sleep, my food intake, and eliminating stress were all top priorities in order to minimise the seizures as best we could.

I managed to grow and learn with my beautiful wife and it was an eye-opening experience. I started off thinking that doctors know best, but the truth of the matter is you are only as good as the information that you acquire (or the doctor sitting across from you). This still is a major part of my journey today, as we seek information from world-leading specialists in order to find something to rid me of my cancer. Sounds quite straightforward, but having to choose which information to pursue is quite complex as ever-evolving technology and discoveries generate some serious questions.

I've said at a few of my presentations that I wouldn't change my original diagnosis. It's quite a bold statement, to which most would wave off thinking, "He has lost his mind." But it's completely true. It has taught me how to really live my life and prioritise what's important to me, not what's important to society. See, there have been some huge lessons for me as to whom or what you let control your life. The truth of my story is learning about myself. Taking lots in my stride, learning about the areas of my life where I am extremely weak and the areas where I am strong and making the most of my life with the people that are dearest to me.

> It has taught me how to really live my life and prioritise what's important.

I have mentioned my wife a few times in this story, but the fact of the matter is that she's everywhere in it. It's the two of us battling through life together as happy as we can be despite the restrictions my health places on us. She's an amazing person and that twinkle I saw in her eye when we first got together, I still see today. Without her, I wouldn't be here. End of story. She gets affected by everything that goes on in my health journey. The ups and downs, the bills and paperwork, the direction in life that she goes in because it's to my advantage. I've been super-privileged to have someone alongside me that backs me 100% and supports me in every way possible.

I am not sure how I can explain in depth the level of thoughts and processing I have been through. For example, the pain I feel that I inflict on loved ones by hindering them from living out their dreams due to my illness is hard to take day after day. Sometimes I feel like an inconvenience and some days it's plain to see. I only wish for people to be happy and I have given my wife plenty of chances to go about fulfilling her life without me, but her loyalty has never wavered for one second. The truth is it is not my decision what choices she makes and she is a testament to the quality of a partner I chose at the start. She is still here today, bending over backwards to help find a cure or get me through the day.

It is a truly wonderful journey that has been undertaken up until now and I can certainly say my life is on track to show the world what life is really all about! So, let's get started on my new understandings in prioritising life. First off, my philosophy on life is this – own it through balance.

We all have our own set of eyes and perceptions, so take whatever information you can and understand it for yourself. At the end of the day, to make the best decision you can, it has to be your own. The buck stops with you. For example, when I was being micro-managed with everything I ate, I began to feel fear if I was eating something that a family member thought wasn't good for me. Let's get this straight though, my family absolutely treasure me, but it became hard when I was the main focus and everyone was preparing meals for me.

Ultimately, this led me to take ownership of my own life. This was the only way that I could remove the fear that surrounded me day to day. This process was a tough lesson to learn. Helping me through that process was an energetic healer named Tamara. Sounds weird, and certainly something I would have never even thought twice about doing before, but the end result was that she started me off with simple questions which exposed my own wounds that hadn't healed (trauma). This was a massive turning point for my emotional and mental health. After constant input from Dr G and such fantastic guidance, I have been able to slowly chip away at myself to become the man I need to be… me!

The constant practice of this new-found knowledge has allowed me to take small steps to holistic living and become the love and light where darkness and fear is all consuming. The outcome of this has been something of a major transition. I actually started a joke, calling myself "baby Jesus"… But I now refer to myself as unicorn_bourne@ instagram because I am a rare, mystical creature that is magical. I can't even

> Become the love and light where darkness and fear is all consuming.

keep a straight face with that, but in the end it's something that I treasure because it's my mantra to do anything and become the first person to survive this cancer. In my thinking, I will not die from the cancer; it will never be the end of me. My life presence is what I cherish most and it can never be taken away. Obviously the underlying moral of my story is this: learn how to find happiness even in the most undesirable of circumstances.

I feel, on reflection now, that my life prior to becoming sick was very much being part of the rat-race. Striving to build a nest egg and get ahead. Looking forward though now, I struggle to apply my old perspectives to this new set of eyes I have. I believe that I have something great to give by sharing my story, and the more positive feedback I get, the more it propels me into wanting to share it even further. I have found that sharing what I have been through has given inspiration to my loved ones as well as people I randomly meet. The flow-on effects have been nothing but positive in nearly all aspects and the growth that I receive as a person has been immeasurable.

Too many things in this life are over-complicated and they don't need to be. Just starting from the start and learning to love yourself is the most important step to true happiness. It's cliché and cheesy, but it's true. Society throws pressure and stress at us from every angle and it blurs our perception of what we are truly about. We didn't get this beautiful opportunity in this life to waste it stressing on stuff in the future or past. We got this opportunity to love and embrace all the special qualities that make us human.

I am about to celebrate not only turning thirty-one, but to celebrate three years of survival from a terminal disease. I found my own new trial in July last year as my body had become resistant/weak to the trial drug and my tumours were growing at a rate of 25% in between three-month scans. This meant that I got told, "You should seek palliative care". Well I say, "F*** that!" Rach and I had already been finding and starting natural options. I started a new trial down in Sydney, which was specialised for me. At the start of any trial, they require baseline scans. Rach and I have learnt to place little importance on these due to the anxieties and pressures it has had on us in the past. The doctor we were dealing with was genuinely interested in what we had been doing as at the next test, because the tumours were the same size as the last scan.

Ultimately where I am now on my journey is a result of all the hard work both myself and my support team have put in. I've gone on to have a tumour removed from my abdomen wall so that I can sleep on my tummy again and spoon my wife. I've also had a haemorrhoid removed which was a result of trial drug side-effects and had affected my quality of life greatly. Remember, I am a terminal case in the medical world, so those operations are not the usual for patients. But I am healthier, stronger and more full of life than I have ever been.

I would like to share with those of you reading this, that life is about *you* and what you see, not what everyone else sees. Hopefully next time you see me it will be in person (with a smile) or on TV in a racing car, or sharing the love on social media or just by a chance meeting. Grab life with both your hands, because it can only be you that can bring yourself happiness. Others can help, but in the end it all comes down to you.

unicorn_bourne@instagram
www.facebook.com/bournetoturnunicorn

Angela Williams

Fearless for Freedom's Sake: From self-discovery to selfless crusader

OUR FIRST CONNECTION

As I sat at a women's event one night, I listened as a very passionate woman shared her desire to save women and girls from a life of addiction and sexual slavery. She really caught my interest and I was very moved as she spoke about the circumstances of some of the women she had helped. I understood, as I too had been caught up in addiction and had met many women in the AA meeting rooms who ended up in sexual slavery to maintain their drug addiction. As soon as the meeting was finished, Angela said she would be waiting at her stall to sell products to raise money for her charity, Her Freedom, which she was now running in Australia. I was one of the first ones out there to meet this fascinating lady. That day, I knew our paths would somehow cross again. How could they not? Angela and I were both passionate about the same cause - using our journeys to bring freedom to others and to change lives for good. This is her story of self-discovery and selfless actions...

Edward Burke once said this: *"All that is necessary for the triumph of evil is for good men to do nothing."* It was this drive to make a difference with my life and do something, anything, about the world's problems that finally gave me the courage to walk into the red-light area one life-changing night, armed with just a tuna sandwich and a hot flask.

I was young, naïve and had never known life in a world where dangers lurked on every corner and darkness embraced you like a heavy coat. A daunting world where you trust no one and no one trusts you. Despite the uncertainty of this unimaginable hell, there was an element of intrigue and adventure that crept beneath the surface of my skin that night. I was finally doing something outrageous, living life on the edge, taking risks and knowing what it really means to be alive.

Until then, I had only ever known a life surrounded by luxury and privilege. As a daughter of a Lord and one of the wealthiest men in Britain, I am not an alien in high-class society. I have lived in the biggest mansion in the area, travelled to exotic locations, flown in private jets, floated on the turquoise waters of the Caribbean Sea and had the latest sports cars. I know how to present myself to the top brass, the rich and famous and the country's leaders. I had grown up in this world; it was home to me. I had been taught my P's and Q's so eloquently in private school. It was only on occasion I'd forget my refined decorum, like walking barefooted through the House of Lords at my father's big inauguration ceremony, surrounded by party leaders, Lords and MP's, while carrying my ill-fitting, toe-pinching, sky-scraping shoes. Vanity was not my friend on this occasion.

I know how it feels to walk into a room and have all eyes stare at you in acknowledgement of who you are and how much wealth your family has, never having seen or met them before. We were show pieces to the curious, who fantasised about how perfect life must be when your bank account has an inexhaustible supply of money. By now you are probably curious yourself as to how and why, when I had the whole world at my feet and every opportunity at my fingertips, did I end up in the red-light area, surrounded by pimps and prostitutes? What on earth convinced me to go there? Isn't this a world that people are trying to escape from? And don't I already live in the world everyone is trying to find?

It was a common misconception throughout my adolescence that because of my lifestyle and my good Christian family values, I was simply too lucky to have a real clue about normal life and living in the real world. Despite whether this was true or not, it automatically disqualified me from ever truly being a part of other people's lives, except for a few close friends. If, on a very rare occasion, we were ever invited into someone's home, it usually began with an apology like, "I am sorry, our house is only small." It was as if they thought that was all that mattered to us.

My perception was that people seemed to be nervous around us. It was as if our presence made others somehow feel less important and less valuable, simply because they were measuring their personal value against our success and wealth, an unfair fight to say the least. The fight for significance lies within all of us - the only difference is how we define significance. Many foolishly believe that significance comes with financial success and having the biggest house, the best car and more money than you can spend. When financial success becomes the measuring stick for significance, then it shows itself in one of two reactions - awe or intimidation. Those in awe would trip over themselves trying to please you and those intimidated by your success would objectify everything you do as if their disapproval justified their dissatisfaction at their own position in life.

> The fight for significance lies within all of us.

Over the years, I became frustrated at this huge divide between the so-called 'us and them', the gap between the "haves and the have-nots", a gap that, despite my best efforts, I couldn't always bridge. I despised the stereotype that "wealthy people only care about their own pleasures and look down their nose at everyone else". Of all the people of wealth I have ever met, I have very rarely seen anyone that fits this unjust label. My father is one of the most humble and generous men I know. He has always accredited his wealth to God's blessing on his life, never taking the credit for himself. He has always seen that his purpose in the prosperity lies in how he can use his wealth to impact the world.

The constant misconception was so far removed from who our family are and how we see the world. People were always too dazzled by the bright lights of what we owned that they were blinded to who we were. I just wanted others to see us for the genuine people we really were at heart and not judged by the outward appearance. There is a scripture in the Bible that has always been a kind of mantra for me throughout my life, a guide to which I live by. It says: *"to whom much is given, much is required"*. I have always had this sense of responsibility. I knew from an early age that my life was meant for far more than just pleasure; that I have a mission to fulfil. I always knew that I had been immensely blessed in my life and therefore a day would come when much more was required of me.

That day finally came on a cold, dark autumnal evening when I arrived in Manchester City in the UK. I was now a wife and a mother to a two-year-old son. Myself and two other friends had been invited for the night to join an outreach project called Barnabas, run by a reformed ex-pimp now working with the homeless and prostitutes of inner-city Manchester. It is a large industrial town well known for its violence and crime. We were invited to experience their outreach as a research mission.

We had been instructed to meet a man called Peter at a certain time and location. So, we jumped into a taxi and gave the driver the address. He took one look up and down at the three finely dressed, well groomed, respectable young women and took another look at the address. He looked again at us and then again at the address before finally saying, "Ahem, are you certain this is the address where you're going?"

We said, "yes that's the address we've been given".

"Well, okay then," he said cautiously and began to drive.

We were chatting in the back seat excitedly about finally living life on the edge and doing something risky for the first time, when suddenly, the taxi came screeching to a halt and the driver said abruptly, "This is as far as I'm going, I won't take you any further. But where you need to be is over there," and he pointed to the other side of this long, dark tunnel that went under a railway station. We jumped out of the car, paid the taxi and he took off as quickly as his foot could reach the pedal.

We stood there completely alone in the darkness of the night looking through this long, dimly-lit, spooky tunnel, not really knowing what awaited us at the other end. We all went silent for a moment. The reality of what we were about to do suddenly hit. As the risks became real and I looked headlong down the tunnel, I did the only one thing I knew how to do. I prayed. "Dear Lord, I know that I am not here by accident, that there is a purpose in what I am about to do in leaving my safe world to enter this dark world where it feels like You don't exist. Be with us now Lord, give us the courage to face this reality without fear and the strength to withstand all that we are about to witness. Give me boldness Lord I pray, in Jesus' name, Amen."

From the moment we entered the tunnel, it felt as though the darkness enveloped us and swallowed us in. When we reached the halfway point, we began to see a large crowd of big burly men forming at the other end. The closer we got, the bigger the crowd grew. Fear tried to paralyse me when they suddenly caught sight of us. Three strange women walking their way, who were clearly not from around here, as no one willingly walked through this tunnel at this time of night. Having a vivid imagination in this moment was really not helpful, as thoughts raced through my mind of the unnerving conversations they were likely having about us: "Oh look guys, here comes some fresh meat," or "You take the blonde one, I'll have the brunette and we'll leave the redhead for dessert."

There was meant to be a white van waiting at the end of the tunnel, where Peter our guide would be waiting. There was no sign of the van and no sign of Peter. Suddenly a boldness came over us just as we'd prayed for and we confidently marched up to the crowd of men and said, "We're looking for Peter."

There came a unanimous call out, "I'm Peter, I'm Peter," as they all fell about laughing. Just at that moment, the white van appeared and out jumped the real Peter to our rescue. These men were the homeless, who were also waiting for the white van that would be feeding and clothing them that night.

Driving through the dark industrial streets of the red-light area, I saw women who were so painfully thin, bruises up and down their bodies, hair all matted, teeth black and missing, lesions and injection marks covering their pale and withdrawn skin. Seeing these women hiding in the shadows of deserted buildings was so heartbreaking and it is to this day, one of the most disturbing scenes I have ever witnessed. This was no Julia Roberts movie, this was real life and I was really there, frozen in disbelief. Do people really live like this? This was nothing like a world I had ever seen, and it instantaneously sobered me up from my comfortable bubble and brought my whole life into perspective.

> Seeing these women hiding in the shadows of deserted buildings was so heartbreaking.

Then it happened! That life-defining moment when I had a collision with destiny and everything changed. I came face to face with my first ever prostitute. Andrea was her name and I will never forget her as long as I live. She stood there with her hands on her hips, barely dressed, looking deathly sick and desperately rattling for her next fix. Aggressively tapping her foot, she scanned me up and down and quickly surmised that I had no idea what I was doing and I was completely clueless about her life. Innocence radiated off my face.

So, with attitude in her voice she shuffled up to me and said, "You've got a pretty face, fancy some work?" and she laughed such a haunting laugh that sent shivers down my spine. She was trying to shock me, knowing I was an easy target for her amusement. As her shock tactics continued, she began to open up quite freely about her life. I was trying desperately not to appear overwhelmed as she talked about rape and abuse so glibly, like an everyday occurrence, and instead I tried to appear understanding. However, with every word, everything within me felt like I was being scratched with sharp nails until she finally put the last nail in my calm resolve when she told me that just two days before, she had given birth to a baby girl. I struggled to believe how she was out here on the streets again, less than forty-eight hours later, selling her body for that small evil powder they call heroin.

I tried to absorb her words and hold back the tears, but an arrow pierced my heart at that moment as a desperate cry for help silently called out from within her and was amplified within me. Destiny knocked on the door of my heart and I knew in that moment that my purpose in life was to rescue women like Andrea for her future and the generations that follow. All my assumptions that they choose this life and can therefore choose to leave were shattered in that moment as I saw for myself how trapped they are in this perpetual cycle of work and drugs. My eyes had been opened and I was no longer the same. I couldn't just return to my life of luxury and feel comfortable about it.

This moment bought me to a crossroads in my life. I could either do nothing or do something. To do nothing was the easiest and safest option, but I knew that I could no longer be satisfied with myself if I did nothing. I was therefore propelled into

> I could no longer be satisfied with myself if I did nothing.

action. I returned to my home town of Coventry, England and did exactly what we'd done in Manchester. I got in my car one day with Maxine, the same friend that came to Manchester, and together we drove into the red-light area with nothing but a tuna sandwich and a hot flask for protection.

We began simply by stopping and talking to the girls while they were working and asking if they wanted a warm drink and something to eat. They were very sceptical of us at first as you don't ever get something for nothing in the world they were used to. We were too good to be true. It took many attempts, night after night, week after week, to gain their trust. But eventually they began to come to the car and see what we were offering.

We continued this service for two hours every Monday night of every week come rain, snow, hail or shine. We were there always and consistently. We made sure we were reliable and fulfilled everything we promised. Eventually we began to make progress and build connections with these women and girls. We formed a charity called Embrace and soon word was on the street that we were here, and here to stay.

We grew in numbers extremely quickly as a variety of people offered to volunteer and join our team. We had everyone on board, from pensioners to popstars. We were a smorgasbord of different flavours from all walks of life, all united in our longing to find purpose and meaning in helping others. Our increase in numbers enabled our services to grow too. We were able to deliver food parcels, do home visits, have drop-in centres, support groups and facilitate excursions. We learnt many valuable new skills and many lessons along the way.

In all the euphoria of the success we were seeing, there were also many challenging and heartbreaking moments that came along too. It was devastating to our team when a girl would suddenly disappear without a trace, only to hear that she had died of drug-related causes or been kidnapped or murdered. Grief would echo through Embrace as we mourned their loss. The dangers became a normal and acceptable part of life for these women, as did the social rejection. It was not uncommon for us to stop and see women who were covered from head to toe in eggs which had been thrown from a passing car while the perpetrators shouted their abuse and accusations.

This dangerous mission required a very quick and steep learning curve for me and I had to grow street-wise very quickly. There were many times where I felt completely out of my depth. In particular, the night one of the "boyfriends" (pimps) was stabbed to death ten times with a twelve-inch blade. Our team had been the last to speak with him as, like any normal Monday evening, he sipped his hot chocolate and ate his cheese sandwich. Not knowing this was the last conversation he would ever have before turning the corner and meeting his death just steps away from where Embrace stood. I had to deal with police questioning and investigations and was thrown in the deep end on many occasions, but God remained my source of strength and wisdom throughout.

I learnt to never lose my cool or break my resolve, for the sake of all the people that were putting their trust in me to keep them safe as they served Embrace. My faith in God became my anchor and my rock, as He gave me the courage to stand up in the face of adversity and to not give up when things got tough. In all this time, I chose to keep my identity private as it made no difference to their life or mine. And besides, this was surprisingly the one place in the world where I was finally known for who I was and not what I had. I was simply Angela, a friend.

It wasn't long before our progress began to draw attention, not just from volunteers but from the local council and others service providers too. The council approached us to ask what they could do to help us. We didn't have to bid for any money, yet they provided the finances for us to buy our own minibus for the women. Despite my lack of knowledge and experience, we were seeing results where others weren't, and they kept asking us what our secret was. I hadn't been trained in drug services, taken self-defence classes or even read the 101 guide to life on the streets, yet we saw success because we were able to offer them something they hadn't experienced before. To be loved with no agenda.

All they truly need to escape this life is the belief that they are worth more and they only discover this when they are loved for the person they are, beyond the lifestyle. To truly be seen beyond the grave clothes of drugs and prostitution is what made us unique and brought us success. Seeing the beauty in people beyond their lifestyle, beyond their choices and beyond their mess is one of the most valuable gifts you can give a person. Whether they live in a mansion or a mud hut, whether they wear Louis Vuitton or Cotton On. When we believe in someone that does not believe in themselves it empowers them to take back their lives and make a positive change.

> When we believe in someone that does not believe in themselves it empowers them.

Embrace is now in its eleventh year and still going strong serving the women of Coventry, UK and changing lives. This charity has brought more purpose and meaning to my life than the latest car or the biggest house ever could. It can no longer be said that I don't understand the real world, for I have walked in the darkest of worlds and loved those the world has rejected. I count many of them as my closest and most dearly-loved friends. The gaping divide between rich and poor, the 'haves and the have-nots', the princesses or the prostitutes, only exists if we give it power by judging the outward appearance and failing to see the value of the person that lies beneath the surface.

These days I spend time advocating for charities in support of women and sharing my story by speaking out publicly.

angela@angelawilliams.info
www.angelawilliams.blog

Stephen Dale

Bouncing Back When You Hit Rock Bottom: From devastating accident to motivational leader

OUR FIRST CONNECTION

Dynamic Dale is what I would call him. Determined and certainly not defeated. His story looked incredible on the email I randomly received from a man who wanted to use his story to inspire school students. I was working in one of the largest state schools in Queensland as a chaplain and we had many boys who were off the rails at the time and needed some guidance. I thought there would be no better than Stephen Dale to come in and share his daring story of survival and resilience after climbing to the top of a cliff on Philip Island and falling almost to his death on the rocks below. Being bullied when he was younger was what had led him to the extreme behaviour and was the catalyst for the accident that day. Many of the boys at school were experiencing problems with bullying and Steve's story inspired and challenged many, including me. So much so that there was no question I would invite him to share his story to inspire a much wider audience. So it came to be that he shared his journey of the utmost bravery with us at Stories of HOPE...

When people hear my story, they often ask me three questions. The first two tend often to arrive at the same time: "Stephen, honestly, why did you climb that cliff? You had to know that you would fall?"

I take a deep breath, prepare to respond, but know that the second question, the *real* question is on its way… "I mean, were you trying to kill yourself?" There you go. Everyone wants to know the answer to *that* question. I give them a smile and know that at any moment they morph into every authoritarian figure of my chequered history.

"I mean, it couldn't have been the accident you say it was," the wannabe psychiatrist continues. "There has to be something else in play, something more sinister." They tilt their head, raise their eyebrows, peer over the rims of their half-glasses, "Hmm? You had been drinking, Stephen, and it sounds like you were an alcoholic. But that, by itself, seems to be a result of your issue, but not the direct cause of your so-called *accident*." Ah yes, here comes the accusing stare of the local constable. "Do you have anything to say about that?" This time, I reply with a typical quip: "Hey. I'm Irish-German, what chance did I have?"

"Be serious, Stephen," I'm warned, this time by my substitute parent, "you also had an unacceptable level of illegal drugs in your system, no tread on the soles of your shoes due to months of hitchhiking down the east coast of Australia in an attempt to 'find yourself', decided to climb a steep, wet cliff in a deserted area, just to get the approval of two strangers? There seems to be a hidden agenda behind your madness."

"Who knows why young men do anything?" I say, trying to calm down the situation.

"That's not good enough. Stephen," says the wannabe headmaster as he raises the imaginary cane above my outstretched hand. I tune out as they continue the blah of their little psychological theory. I cannot help but wonder why people would rather find a reason that suits them, rather than listen to the answer.

The truth is, I know the exact reason why I made that dreadful, selfish decision. I know why I was so deeply into my depressive world that I was willing to run the risk of losing my own life and nearly destroy the lives of two innocent witnesses. I wasn't trying to top myself; I was trying to impress them. I tried, no, *needed* to impress *everybody*, and do you want to know why? I was not enough.

Somewhere along the way, I chose to believe that lie. As far back as I remember, I have always felt that I am not enough for anyone to like me for being just as I am. I was not *enough*. Believing in that lie makes zero sense.

> I was not *enough*. Somewhere along the way, I chose to believe that lie.

I was adored by my parents. The first twelve years of my life were so textbook that Disney should base all family films on my idyllic childhood and near-perfect parents. We made the Brady Bunch look like the Manson family.

But whatever the reason, I adopted that lie with such fervour and obsession that it became my undeniable truth. I forced that lie to seep into my DNA like a carnivorous virus. I was not *enough* for you to play with me. I was not *enough* to be your friend. I certainly was not *enough* for you to love me. If you are interested in finding out why I made the decision to climb that sheer, slippery, algae-blackened cliff, that's the answer. It's the same reason I became dependent on alcoholic relief and the energy of amphetamines. That is why I ran away from Brisbane. That is why I tried so hard to become someone, anyone else. I wanted to be *enough*.

Maybe the acceptance of that lie was pre-natal. My incessant squirming during delivery wrapped the umbilical cord two-and-a-half times around my scrawny little neck and strangled my tiny self. My high anxiety caused me to vomit the contents of my ballooning belly, but I could not. The tightening umbilical noose blocked the airway, causing the acid to burn, blistering my little insides. Perhaps it was the hysteria of yanking my little body out of my traumatised mother and leaving me to rot in a dark, cold, silent chamber, where they fed me with a sterile eye-dropper, making me an untouchable and unhuggable alien for the first three weeks of my pathetic little life.

It may have been from the horrific, yet highly creative bullying at school, which continually smashed into my little brain that no one wants me. I will never have friends. I am awful. I deserve to die a slow, bloody and painful death. Maybe it was those teenage girls who pretended to be interested in my skinny, bony and formless self, only to make me a laughing stock in front of a jeering crowd.

Perhaps it was when I finally discovered my true gift in life. I could drink men twice my size under the table without looking or sounding like I'd had a drop. I could drink all night, tee off at dawn, hit the ball straight down the middle of the fairway, and never suffer a hangover. While my "friends" are heaving, suffering and vowing to never drink again, I am busy buying the greasiest, messiest burger and enjoying eating it in front of them as they are bent over with sickness. Tough to choose when that lie became my personal truth when faced with such a treasure of riches.

So, when an employer in Brisbane offered me to continue to work for him in Sydney, I answered him before he even finished the question. I would tell everyone that I "wanted to live my own life for a while," but I knew that as soon as I left this filthy city, I was never going to return. Never. When I told the people who allowed me to hang out with them the news, they were happy for me. I mean, really, *really* happy that I was going.

Now, just in case you've never been to Sydney, it is probably not the best place to go if you have a blossoming alcohol and drug habit. Nor might it be the best choice if you are terribly lonely and aching for a friend. As the story goes, I only lasted in Sydney a few months until I needed to leave, or should I say run, to a safer, kinder place. Two terrible cities in a row? Gee, I'm unlucky. I was sure that Melbourne will be the place that wraps its arms around me.

When I ran away from Melbourne, still amazed with my string of bad luck cities, I realised that Tasmania would be the place I would settle for a while. I had heard that Tasmanians are a bit slow, but are nice, simple people, so I should fit right in.

When I had to leave Tasmania, I was a little confused about where to go. I didn't want to go to Adelaide. It really was too far away, too hot, too small for me to hide and I only had two dollars and fifteen cents to my name, so I decided to head back to Melbourne. It was a huge city; so as long as I stayed on the other side of Melbourne, there was only little chance I would bump into unwanted acquaintances, so off I went.

I talked my way into a job working behind the bar of a fancy restaurant and discovered that my most loyal friends, Johnny Walker, Jim Beam and Jack Daniels, also worked there. We made sure that we were always on the same shifts as each other and enjoyed each other's company immensely. We also made sure that we worked double, or even triple shifts every day, seven days a week. Oh, we had some great times, many of which I can hardly remember.

There were also parties at the end of each night's work, and incredibly enough I found two human friends. Rob and Dave weren't binge drinkers or drug lovers and seemed to have too much inner peace for us to have any common ground, but they seemed to like me and I decided not to talk them out of it. They only worked five days a week, so on the weekends they had "adventures". The next adventure was on Phillip Island. They invited me to join them to have some "fun" on this "adventure".

I wanted to know their definitions of "fun" and "adventure" before I made any commitment. I had been tricked in Sydney, so having fun and going on adventures required more information. I was too under-slept and over-medicated to run the risk of any unlawful activity that would take more energy than my pills could provide. "Adventures", I was informed, was "going to a place they haven't been before and doing whatever they wanted."

"Fun" means fishing, snorkelling, spear-fishing, swimming and maybe meeting some new girls.

That sounded fine, but it did not include drinking, doing drugs, or fighting. I wasn't sure how you could have fun without a drink in your hand, a pill in your pocket and a fist ready to throw at a passing jawline, but hanging out with some decent individuals would actually be an adventure, regardless of the definition. Besides, my boss was getting suspicious about the sudden disappearances of all the Johnnies, Jimmies and Jackies - most usually on my shift.

So, we left early the following morning, fished and swam (had a few drinks when we stopped off for a counter lunch, so the day wasn't a total waste) and ended up at a deserted little spot called Pyramid Rock, where I secretly dropped whatever chemical pleasure was lurking in my sweatpants pocket. Thankfully, I have no actual memory of what happened next, so David Smith will take the story from here...

It was a warm/hot day and we checked out a few beaches before deciding to go to Pyramid Rock as a potential fishing/spear-fishing location. The beach was very rocky surrounded by steep cliffs, especially on the southern side.

We generally messed around, throwing rocks, skimming stones etc. before Steve and I decided to climb over the southern cliff to get to view the main pyramid rock. The first fifteen to twenty metres was just solid rock, lots of foot and hand holds, but after this, it became more of a steep hill, no vegetation and mostly loose, crumbly dirt.

After completing this part, I started up a small dirt track. I slipped a couple of times and there was nothing to grab, so I felt very uneasy as there was probably twenty metres of this stuff to climb until it was safe.

Steve was still coming up the rock face at this stage and after noticing I had stopped, Steve called me a bit of a wimp, which I didn't appreciate. I explained the loose rocks and suggested going back. Steve went on climbing right past me. I really didn't want Steve to make it to the top as I'd have to follow. I heard an "uh oh". I turned to see Steve slipping down on his stomach, legs pedalling madly and arms reaching to get some sort of hold, but there was none. It was probably only a split second before Steve came within an arm's reach of me. By this time, the "uh oh" had changed to an "aargh!" as Steve quickly slid past me a metre or so away.

I didn't watch Steve go over the edge; I consciously turned my head away so that I didn't have to watch. In some funny way, I hoped that I would turn around and see Steve hanging by his fingernails, like some silly movie and I could pull him up – but it wasn't to be. I heard the thud of his body hitting the rocks at the bottom of the cliff. It was a horrible, horrible sound that I don't ever want to hear again. I can't describe it any more than to say that I knew Steve would not be sitting there with a broken leg or something so minor – it was clear his whole body hit very hard.

It took about two minutes to climb down to Steve. He was still very much alive. He was on his stomach with his head lodged between two boulders. Blood was starting to flow from Steve's ears, nose and mouth as well as somewhere around his skull. The blood from his right ear soon turned into what looked like brain fluid. His breathing was very strained and all we could do was look at Steve and think about what to do.

We agreed to pull Steve back onto the rock, and checked him over as best and as quickly as we could. I checked his skull, neck, back, arms, chest and legs for breaks as well as having a general poke and prod. From what I could figure, Steve had badly fractured his skull in a couple of places, his neck wasn't blatantly out of place, but didn't feel good, his back had about three spots in it which was mush, I thought complete breakage, and his ribcage was very fluid in a couple of spots. The blood coming from his mouth and nose was foamy, so I assumed he also fractured ribs and at least one punctured lung. I also assumed other internal injuries were on the list, certainly way beyond the scope of two first aiders with no equipment.

We made a decision that whilst we couldn't do anything about the breaks, if we continued to do nothing, Steve would bleed to death. I took off my Thunderbirds singlet and wrapped it around his head, trying to incorporate as best as possible the parts that were bleeding the most. I covered one part of his head and watched the blood come from his ears, then tried to cover that to see the blood coming from his nose. In the end, Steve got wrapped up like a mummy and my singlet went from white to red very quickly.

Steve stopped breathing and soon after that, his heart stopped. At this point, the shock wore off both of us and we got into action. Rob just started doing mouth to mouth and all I could immediately think was how many breaths to how many cardio massages. Neither of us could remember, so I think we started with fifteen and two. In the end I think both of us just kept doing something and that was the important part.

Every time I depressed his broken rib cage during heart massage, I wondered if I was just adding to the punctures in his lungs. But the words of my first aid instructor came to me: "If you do nothing, the person could die. If you break their ribs or puncture a lung the person would still stand a chance of living." It was all I had to cling on to. We continued CPR for ages (maybe it was an hour, I don't know) and got into some sort of rhythm. Steve's heart stopped several times (maybe five), and each time was for longer and longer.

I wondered what the next step was as we had two problems. Firstly, Steve was on a rock that was very near to the water's edge and the tide was coming in. We had only an hour or so before we would be working on Steve in the water, unless he was moved. We didn't want to move him as I was sure he at least had a broken back. Secondly, we were in a remote area. We had seen no one in the last hour or so. If no one came, someone would have to go for help.

We decided not to decide. We wouldn't move him until the very last moment and we weren't going to split up and try to get help until he had stabilised, if that was possible. The next timeframe was really a blur. I remember people turning up in coloured suits and just taking over the CPR. They didn't ask much, just got busy trying to clean Steve up and one calling the air ambulance. They put a neck brace on Steve and he was moved onto a stretcher.

I spoke to an ambo, who sort of complimented us but also tore us apart at the same time, by telling us that we'd done a great job reviving Steve and keeping him alive, but he was most likely going to be a vegetable and perhaps we "shouldn't have revived him." That was the first time I had given that any consideration. We'd worked hard to give Steve life and I was angry that someone should tell us that we'd made the wrong decision. Anger quickly turned to fear as we sat down to think about the events that had just transpired, as was so for many weeks to come, as Steve lay in a coma.

It took a while for the emergency crew to discover my identity. I had done all I could to become as anonymous and nameless as possible. When they did find out, it wasn't easy to track down anyone who would admit they were family. These poor people were the next victims of my selfish and brainless decision.

My sister Kathy Oldman recalls...

It had just been an ordinary Saturday afternoon in Brisbane and my husband Mal and I planned to spend a relaxing evening at home. At 6 p.m., Mal took a call and I watched his facial expressions become more and more serious. What was wrong? What had happened? Just get off the phone and tell me!

My brother Steve had been involved in a serious climbing accident and was in a critical condition with multiple injuries. It was imperative that the next of kin get to the hospital in Melbourne ASAP.

That 11.30 p.m. flight was the worst few hours of my life. The words, "We don't expect him to survive the night," terrified me and sent constant waves of panic and nausea.

When I arrived at the hospital and was finally allowed to see Steve, I did not recognise him. His head was so swollen, lacerated and bruised. His brain was placing more pressure on his expanding skull fractures. Brain fluid was leaking from his right ear, therefore leading to a greater risk of further damage and infection.

Added to this, he had also dislocated his spine from his hips, and sheared five bones off his lower vertebrae. Any wrong move would result in paralysis. His liver, kidneys, lungs and stomach had each been badly damaged. His sternum, ribs, cheek, nose and jaw were also badly fractured and they could not control his internal bleeding. His right hand was smashed and had swollen to twice its normal size. His face, arms, legs, chest and back were severely lacerated, with dirt and rocks buried deeply in his wounds. A huge deep black bruise covered his entire right-hand side, but he was still alive.

I stood by his bedside and wished that he would open his eyes and give me some sign that he would live, but nothing happened. Was he aware of what had happened? Did he know I was there?

My father Rodney Dale recalls…

I asked the doctors of his possibility of recovery and whether Steve would suffer any long-term deficits. The doctor explained that Steve had suffered serious, multiple injuries throughout his body and brain. He explained that in all his time in emergency, he had never seen anything like this. Their chief concern was with the possible development of meningitis from brain infection. It was then that tears welled in his eyes as he softly spoke of Steve's brain injury, which would have irreversible consequences.

Quite often, when people hear the word coma, they picture the blissful and serene Hollywood coma. You know the one I mean, where the victim wears perfect makeup, has beautifully manicured hair and lies serenely on an ergonomic bed while the expensive bedside machine goes *bing!* in conjunction with the beating of their peace-filled heart? Yes, that one. Perhaps my sister Kathy sheds a better light…

Even though he was still unconscious, his body thrashed about, having continual and violent spasms. For the sake of his own safety, the staff gave Steve an entire ward, covered wall to wall in mattresses. Steve frequently ripped out his catheter and the drip in his arm, so someone needed to be with him at all times. The other problem was that Steve could be very aggressive with the male nurses, so he was placed in shackles.

Dad and I watched Steve around the clock. As Steve thrashed around the room, I would follow him, wheeling his drip, while Dad would often crawl after him and whisper, "You fight this," over and over again in his ear. One thing that stays in my mind is Steve's incredible physical strength, even though he was unresponsive. For someone who had suffered such horrific injuries, he was still able to move around with brute force, smashing over anything or anyone who stood in his way. His movements threatened his fragile spine, but he would not stop. To be near Steve was a threat in itself.

On one occasion, he needed medical attention and several male staff members were required to hold him still, but they were too busy trying to protect each other from Steve's onslaught. Many male staff members would not return to his ward. He was never like that with either Dad or me, nor with any of the female nurses. However, he seemed to have some issue with the male nurses touching him.

When I read Kath's account, I can only think that the memory of being held down and punished by my high school bullies had seeped so far into my DNA, that my broken brain transported to a time when I had to fight for my life, albeit in a very different way. Twelve months, innumerable operations and procedures, constant bad news from doctors, continual firing of such doctors, nightly violent, demon-riddled hallucinations, dozens of shackles broken followed by a desperate man jumping off his bed onto a concrete floor, new x-rays, new breaks discovered, thousands of dirty bed-pans and overflowing urine-bottles, forty-five kilograms of body weight lost, shipments of new syringes, newly invented curse words, the never-ending flame of cold-turkey, installation of a two-inch thick body cast, 100+ sponge baths, 200+ erections (encouraging sign of recovery) and two broken hearts, (both mine, due to unrequited

> Punished by my high school bullies had seeped so far into my DNA.

love from many fine nurses) and four hospitals later, it was time for my parents to decide whether or not to put me in a long-term rehabilitation facility or take me home.

The prognosis was that my brain would not recover sufficiently to get a job or live an independent life. My physical injuries would require constant attention, which I would not be able to monitor correctly. Important to note, *neuroplasticity* was not even a word in 1989 let alone an accepted medical doctrine. The existing dogma insisted that a damaged brain would never heal, so neither would I.

However, my beautiful, loving, God-fearing parents decided to take me home. They are too humble to admit it, but I am certain that they wondered if that was the correct decision every day for the first three years. To say that I was a handful is so ridiculous it's funny. My emotions were limited to three - anger, depression and guilt. They came mostly, but not always, in that order. What was most interesting was when all three emotions came at once. I'm sure an actor with the versatility of Jim Carrey could have managed them, but for me, it was simply unbearable, as was the pain.

Every simple action that I once took for granted led to failure and humiliation. I was told straight to my twisted face on many an occasion and by many an 'expert' that I would never recover and any attempt was futile. One specialist (a specialist in what? I must question...) told my carers that they should stop me from trying to get better. "Steve will only be more disappointed when he fails," they'd said.

My friends soon found it too difficult to come around, and the few who did often left in tears. On one occasion, a girl that I once fancied came to see me and with one look at me, she vomited. Not real good for the male ego, I must add. Everyone, including me, wondered if I would have been better off if David and Rob let me die that day at the base of that cliff. That thought, however, only happened once. Just the thought of David and Rob working so hard to give me life, I wanted to make sure that I wasn't going to throw it away. Any depressive thought was nothing less than a punch in the face to both of those young men. I was not going to fail them.

Every time I thought about my parents, I recalled the heartache and sorrow I so frequently brought them. They had a perfect opportunity to palm me off, but loved me so much that they brought me home, which I can assure you, was no picnic in the park. I would not let them down. I thought of the wonderful nurses in each of my four hospitals. They treated me like I was the most important person in the world. When I had night hallucinations, they held my hand, mopped my sweaty brow and dried my tear-filled eyes. They wiped, cleaned and sometimes mopped up my mess and laughed at my clumsy attempts to tell them I was in love with them. Their effort would not be wasted.

> I wanted to make sure that I wasn't going to throw it away.

Motivating my broken body to surpass every single damned expectation, including my own, became my new obsession. I was going to fight like I had never fought before. I was going to rewrite every medical journal only to regain, and then surpass, all my lost cognitive functions. I would teach myself to speak, read and write better than I could B.C. (code for Before Cliff). I would teach myself how to put on clothes, clean my own teeth, make my own bed and make my own decisions. I would teach myself to walk, catch, jump and swim again. This time, I would stand up for myself. I would fight for my right to live the healthy, happy and love-filled life like the one I had always dreamed of. I had constantly been told that I can't, but this time, I would.

Previously, I was told that I wasn't good/smart/handsome/funny enough to achieve any happiness and yes, I used to believe that lie also. But

> I would stand up for myself. I would fight for my right to live.

not this time. Not ever. It would take some time to overcome these temporary speed-bumps. Even if it took the rest of my life and take gallons of blood, sweat and tears before I reached my new self-appointed potential, I would do it. Even if I was laughed at, mocked, jeered or perhaps humiliated, I would do it. I knew there would be times when I'd have to hide so that I could cry without being seen or heard. And there would be times when I just could not take any more and would want to give in. But I wouldn't.

It may take every ounce of my energy and every grain of willpower for every day for the rest of my life, but one day, I would be victorious. I just clung to one HOPE. It may have been the logic of someone suffering from a brain injury, but it made, and still makes, perfect sense to me: "If I keep trying, every day, every month, year and decade from here on in, I would have to be better at it than I currently am." Sounds simple, and I bet it'll be true.

Little did I know, when I began this new creed in 1990, that I would achieve all those goals and surpass every expectation. It only took me ten years. That's it, just ten. Yes, I failed every attempt in every moment of every day for the first few years, but then, almost unexpectedly, I started failing less often, and actually started succeeding. I wet myself frequently, vomited down the front of every clean shirt that I owned, dirtied every pair of pants on more occasions than I care to recall, but that didn't last either.

My terrible speech impediment faded. My twisted walk straightened. My ability to focus lengthened. My handwriting became legible. My pain lessened. My tolerance grew. My smile beamed. My laugh bellowed. My humour increased. My friendships strengthened. It turned out to be the best ten years of my life.

I once thought that falling off a cliff had to be the worst day of my life, but I now consider it to be the best. If I hadn't fallen off a cliff, I would not have my speaking and mentoring business. I would never have met the wonderful people or seen the beautiful places I have visited. I would never have met, and married, Allison, the one true love of my life. It is because of this event, that I am who I am. And I like who I am.

Oh, and the third question I am often asked? How did I stay so focussed for so long and fight through so much pain and difficulty, when I didn't know if it would pay off? The answer? Because *I am enough.*

www.smilingtiger.com.au

Acknowledgements

A special thank you to the Sands Tavern. You have generously donated us a space to call home each month from the very beginning, and without your support, we wouldn't be able to have the impact and reach in the community that we have. Thank you to all our sponsors who have walked alongside us and supported us in different ways and especially Fritz and Charlotte Radda from DT Rustproofing who have sponsored us financially each month. Thank you for partnering with us to make a difference in this world.

To my husband Marty, who never really realised when he married me the extent to which he would have to share me with the rest of the world: thank you for allowing me the freedom to be myself and for encouraging my passion for helping the lost, broken, downtrodden and lonely to find HOPE and purpose. Together we are a great team, working towards helping others to find that HOPE in an ever-changing world.

To my daughter Aleisha, the only girl in my life who has truly shown me unconditional love: you bring me so much joy and laughter right when I need it. You are wise beyond your years with a rare ability to listen to others and see a situation from all angles without judgement. You have seen the very worst of me and the best of me and have been by my side and shown me support that has known no bounds when I needed it the most. You are the most incredible daughter and friend anyone could ever wish for.

To my son Joshua: we have such a special bond. You bring happiness, vitality and laughter wherever you are and bring an energy into the room that is larger than life. You have been such an incredible rock for me and I have leant on you more than any mum should have to. You have always encouraged me and made me believe that anything is possible. You share the same passion to help the hurting, the lost and lonely, and I am so proud to call you my son.

Thank you to my mum and dad, who are no longer in this world. They taught me what it is to truly love others unconditionally.

To my amazing brothers Carl and Rusty: thank you for all your support and for always being there for me. We will always be the 3 Fishers.

To my son-in-law Joel, the little lights in my life, my granddaughters, Aaliyah and Mia, my extended family and all my friends out there - and there are so many - who have helped me on my journey to form and carry out my vision: friendship means so much to me and I value each and every one of you and your contribution to my life. Especially you Catherine Smith. Thank you. It is because of you all that I am sharpened.

Thank you to all who have assisted me in the process of writing this book. To Alex Smith for the amazing design cover, Roxanne McCarty-O'Kane for your patience, editing skills and expertise with words, and to Alex Fullerton and Sylvie Blair from Author Support Services for helping me with publishing and design to bring the book to life.

To my dear friend Monique Parker, thank you for believing in me and helping me to find my purpose and carry out my vision.

To all my Stories of HOPE family and team of speakers: you have caught a glimpse of my vision and bared your souls in order to change lives and show everyone out there who is going through hard times that they are not alone. You are an inspiration and living proof that not only is there light at the end of the tunnel, but that life and great purpose after tragedy and difficulty is definitely possible: you are the best team ever. Thank you, Stuart Rawlins, for standing beside me on the front line and for always being the voice of encouragement. Thank you Darron

Acknowledgements

Eastwell for all the behind-the-scenes support you have given me. Knowing you all and what you have been through continues to encourage and inspire me on a daily basis to keep running with and expanding my vision to reach as many people out there in the far corners of the earth with this message: together is better and there is always HOPE.

If you have been touched by this book and would like to book a Stories of HOPE event in your town, workplace, corporate event or school, we would love to hear from you. Please visit our website.

www.storiesofhope.com.au
info@storiesofhope.com.au

Look out for the second book in the Stories of HOPE Australia series to read more inspiring stories from remarkable people. Until then, know that whatever you are going through, there is always HOPE.

www.ingramcontent.com/pod-product-compliance
Lightning Source LLC
Chambersburg PA
CBHW050552300426
44112CB00013B/1887